SAVING
DINNER FOR
THE HOLIDAYS

SAVING DINNER FOR THE HOLIDAYS

Menus, Recipes, Shopping Lists, and Timelines for Spectacular, Stress-free Holidays and Family Celebrations

LEANNE ELY

BALLANTINE BOOKS • NEW YORK

*This book is lovingly dedicated
to my children, Caroline and Peter,
who make every day a party
and a celebration.*

CONTENTS

ACKNOWLEDGMENTS

At the heart of every book I've ever written are always the wonderful people around me who have made it all possible: My children, Caroline and Peter, who gave me the time I needed to get the work done—thanks, guys, I love you! My assistant Kandi Speegle, who has helped me enormously with everything from making an appointment with the vet for my dogs to making sure my deadlines were met with my publisher—this woman has schlepped, taken out the trash, and made phone calls on my behalf. Talk about a saint; thank you, Kandi, for *everything*!

Bonnie Schroader's creativity has made our Web site, www.savingdinner.com what it is today. She deserves a standing ovation and oodles of kudos for all her hard work—I am so thankful for you, Bonnie.

My mom, AKA Muzz, made every shopping list in this book, put together timelines, and kept me sane through the whole writing process. She is my biggest fan and I'm her biggest fan, too. You're the best—thanks, Mom!

Marla Cilley, the ever famous FlyLady, continues to be one of the biggest encouragements in my life. This woman is an anchor and a rock, and I'm thankful for her input on everything in my life, professionally and personally. I am blessed to know you, Marla.

My own staff continues to do a stellar job and to them—Nikki and Robyn—a hearty thank you!

To Caroline Sutton, my editor at Ballantine—thank you for your input, brisket recipe tracking, and for straightening me out as needed along the way. Michelle Tessler, my fantastic agent, thank you once again!

INTRODUCTION

In a perfect world, having the holidays at home would be a happy tradition where recipes have been handed down for generations and picture-perfect holiday meals with all the fixings would emerge from the kitchen to thunderous applause from family and friends sitting around appropriately decorated tables.

But it's not like that anymore. Maybe in a Norman Rockwell painting or a rerun of *The Waltons*, but that is fiction; this is real life. Microwaves and drive-thru's intrude on the scene, and now more than ever before, the traditional celebratory meals such as Thanksgiving, Christmas, and other significant holidays are being observed in restaurants, or the food is ready-made from the local grocery store or caterer.

The result? We're left feeling empty and dissatisfied, somehow. These special holidays in our families' lives are relegated to a cold restaurant atmosphere where the cost is more than financial. And yet, bringing the holidays home where we want them seems unattainable and too overwhelming. We don't have the time or the energy to execute the plan—if we even had one.

Enter *Saving Dinner for the Holidays*. It is offered in the same spirit as were *Saving Dinner* and *Saving Dinner the Low-Carb Way*, which were enthusiastically embraced by thousands of people as the answer to the "What's for Dinner?" question. I have taken on the holidays to answer the next question, "How do I do [name the holiday] at home?"

The answers are in this book. As in the first two books, *Saving Dinner for the Holidays* has menus, recipes, and shopping lists. Except in this book, I have added all the extra details you will need to save your holidays: timelines, detailed plans and hints, decorating ideas—the whole enchilada. What you have here is a bona fide tool for making it all happen, at last.

So enough chit-chat already. Let's get busy and start Saving the Holidays!

HOW TO THROW A PARTY, AND PARTY PARTICULARS YOU NEED TO KNOW

Throwing a party is a lot like fly fishing. You need a little finesse, the right touch, and a little know-how. Like the Kenny Rogers song says, "You gotta know when to hold 'em, know when to fold 'em." There are certain things a host or hostess can do to achieve an ambience of fun, laughter, and a really good time.

First, you need to take a chill pill. Don't overdo it, making everything from scratch, decorating from floor to ceiling, and getting everything just "perfect." Perfect, believe it or not, does not help your guests relax and feel at home. Rather, they feel as if they've entered some sort of party spread from a magazine and it's all an illusion. In other words, you want your party "touchable"—something that everyone can participate in, not just observe.

Second, be prepared. I've given you timelines for every party so you don't have to make yourself crazy worrying about the details. Still, that doesn't mean you don't have to think for yourself. There is always plenty to do, even when you're fully prepared.

For most holidays, I don't name the beverage or beverages to be consumed for the evening. Why? This is an area of personal preference and so it is hard to come up with a formula. People pretty much know what they want to do beverage-wise at their parties. Some people choose to serve alcohol; some don't. Some don't mind laboring over drinks, making punches, and so on, as well as the food aspect of hosting a party, but others would rather not. And while the shopping list is already made up for the party, adding a few beverages and a bag of ice or two is no big deal.

That being said, I include a few fun cocktails for some select parties, such as chocolate martinis for the chocolate fest on Valentine's Day and margaritas for the adult birthday bash. The reason I offer drink recipes for only these two parties is to keep the book simple and not overwhelm the party giver. Entertaining, especially if this is something you don't do often, can be downright scary if you take on too much. But it can be a thrill to have people over for a party and a lot of fun when it's taken in bite-size pieces, appropriately accessorized with great shortcuts, easy menus, and some outright cheating. You will see what I mean as you read on.

There are extremely easy decorating ideas in this book as well. They're not overly ambitious and actually pretty elementary. That is done on purpose, too; my book is all about being simple and easy. A few of the holiday chapters have nothing in them decorating-wise (like Graduation—all you need is a nice-looking buffet table with some flowers), but they are in the minority. And remember that these ideas are mere suggestions and you needn't do them if you don't like them.

On another note, you'll find I have used a few of the recipes more than once for different holidays. That's because they're good basics, they hold up well for entertaining, and they are just plain good. It makes perfect sense to reuse recipes when they work well.

SAVING DINNER FOR THE HOLIDAYS

THANKSGIVING

I f holiday meals were royalty, the big Thanksgiving Day meal no doubt would be king. The big turkey is as regal as ever, and the attending side dishes are equally treasured. There is nothing more wonderful than to walk into a home with the smell of a Thanksgiving meal permeating the air.

Having your menu planned in advance is as critical as inviting your guests. Thanksgiving is the embodiment of what the dinner table is all about. It's more than just a big meal. This great feast is a means of tying together the heartstrings of extended family and friends. Having traditions during this holiday meal is one way we can put down anchors for our families and help them understand their place and role in our own family circles. The family dinner table is the day-in, day-out version of this celebratory meal. Thanksgiving takes this concept a step further with its own traditions, and familiar recipes add a distinctiveness to the holiday that are all their own.

At my sister's house, they always have sweet potato casserole with gobs of miniature marshmallows on top, all browned and gooey. One traditional recipe at my house has always been my mom's stuffing recipe (it's the best and—don't worry—it's here!), and another is my own homemade cranberry sauce (that one is here, too).

EASY DECORATING FOR THANKSGIVING

The key in my mind for any holiday is to keep the decorating simple and cost-effective. When I decorate my Thanksgiving table, I use items bearing the colors of the season: miniature pumpkins and seasonal gourds piled up in a basket. I purchase them a few at a time from the grocery store as soon as they start becoming available. Last year, I had a larger sugar pumpkin on either side of the basket with two beeswax taper candles in pewter candlestick holders, just waiting to be lit.

I placed three burnt orange candles of various sizes and heights on the sideboard, all purchased from a discount store. Next to that was a big bunch of dried wheat standing on its own, tied with a raffia bow. The effect was beautiful and without a big price tag. I encourage you to decorate early and start getting in the mood. And though you will need to move some of your festive decorations to put the food on the table come Thanksgiving, you can enjoy your pretty table arrangement now.

The Menu

SIMPLE ROAST TURKEY AND PAN GRAVY

MUZZIE'S FABULOUS STUFFING

ORANGE CRANBERRY SAUCE

OLD-FASHIONED MASHED POTATOES

OVEN-ROASTED SWEET POTATOES AND ONIONS

SAUTÉED GREEN BEANS WITH NUTMEG

ROLLS AND BUTTER

PUMPKIN CHEESECAKE

THE SHOPPING LIST

MEAT

1 15- to 16-pound turkey, fresh or frozen (your choice)

1 pound bulk breakfast sausage (I use Farmer John links with no casings)

CONDIMENTS

Extra-virgin olive oil

PRODUCE

3 pounds onions

4 medium red onions

1 head garlic

1 bunch carrots

1 bunch celery

1 green apple (smallish)

1 bunch parsley

5 pounds russet potatoes (12 medium potatoes)

Fresh green beans (12 good handfuls, LOL)

8 medium sweet potatoes (they are reddish and in the
   West they call them yams, but they are wrong! LOL)
1-pound bag fresh cranberries

CANNED GOODS

1 or 2 (14.75-ounce) cans chicken broth (or more for
   backup)
1 (16-ounce) can pumpkin puree (not pumpkin pie filling)

SPICES

Thyme

Poultry seasoning

White pepper

Sage

Nutmeg

Lemon pepper

Ground cinnamon

Ground ginger

Pure vanilla extract

DAIRY/DAIRY CASE

2 pounds unsalted butter (freeze any remaining)

Heavy cream (¾ cup)

Half-and-half for coffee

Milk (for making potatoes—about 1 cup)

Orange juice (1 cup)

3 (8-ounce) packages Philadelphia cream cheese
   (best brand)

Eggs (4)

DRY GOODS

Wondra flour or Pillsbury's fine flour (they're in canisters and shake out)

Sugar (at least 2 pounds for baking, cranberries, coffee, etc.)

Coffee for dessert (perhaps decaf?)

1 box Mrs. Cubbison's Bread Stuff Mix (on the East Coast, use Pepperidge Farm—*not* the cornbread kind)

1 envelope turkey gravy mix (don't freak out!)

1 box ginger snaps

FROZEN FOODS

Rolls for 12 (good alternative if you don't do bakery rolls)

BAKERY

Rolls for 12 (at my house, that would be 3 dozen!)

TOOLS OF THE TRADE

Check your tools. Do you have what you need? This is all essential equipment. You needn't go out and buy everything—this stuff is all easily borrow-able, just ask!

Turkey baster (if you still want to baste after my basting diatribe)

Meat thermometer (remember, *meat*, not candy thermometer)

Cutting board (there is a place on these boards for the juices to go)

Carving knife set

Large roasting pan (flimsy aluminum ones are a hazard and don't cook the turkey nearly as well as a real roaster—invest in one or borrow one)

Rack for the bottom of the roasting pan

Roll of heavy-duty aluminum foil

Kitchen scissors

Kitchen twine or one of those turkey kits with the skewers and thread (I don't use any of them, but some people like them)

Wire whisk

Potato masher

Electric beaters or mixer

9-inch springform pan (for cheesecake)

Gravy boat (for passing the gravy)

SIMPLE ROAST TURKEY

Serves 12 (with leftovers)

1 15-pound turkey (at least, I will probably go bigger for more
    leftovers)
½ cup unsalted butter, softened
Salt and pepper to taste
1 recipe Muzzie's Fabulous Stuffing (page 14)
(un-stuffing option: 1 carrot, 1 large onion, 1 celery stalk, 1 green
    apple, some thyme, some sage)
Thyme
Sage
Water

You will usually find a package of giblets (innards) in the neck cavity of the turkey. Remove those and place in the fridge; I will tell you what to do with them later. Right now, it's bath time for old tom. Rinse the cavities (the neck and bottom) and outside of the bird with cool water, then pat dry with paper towels. Sprinkle the cavity of the turkey lightly with salt, if desired. (If you are not stuffing the bird, throw a washed carrot cut in half, a large onion cut in half, and a celery stick cut in half into the cavity; sprinkle in a little thyme and some salt and pepper. You can also add half a green seeded apple, quartered if you like. I would also throw a little sage in there, about ½ a teaspoon, and mix everything up with my hand. This will help to flavor the drippings, which in turn will help you make scrumptious gravy.) Do not salt the cavity if you will be stuffing the turkey.

If you will be stuffing the bird, don't do it now. Wait to do that till just before it hits the oven. Remove a rack from the oven, and position the last rack to be on the second to the bottom ledge (in other words, not the very bottom). Turn on the oven to preheat, 500 degrees.

Place the turkey, breast side up, on a rack in a shallow roasting pan (the rack will help the whole turkey brown). Rub your bird down (using your hands) with a cube of softened, unsalted butter (this isn't one of those calorie-conscientious meals). You will want to get under the skin and over the skin, too (unless putting your hand under the turkey's skin creeps you out). Put ½ cup of water in the bottom of the pan. If you are using a meat thermometer (which is advised), place the thermometer in the thickest part of the thigh muscle, but do not allow it to touch the bone or you will get a false reading.

Now, stuff the bird if you are going to stuff it. I have recently become a dressing convert after years of stuffing my bird. I used to stuff and I love the stuffing, but I have found that stuffing the turkey is one of the reasons the turkey dries out, so my stuffing has become dressing. A part of me mourns the loss of that delectable stuffing that came out of my turkey, but the other part of me is thrilled with the moist results of my turkey.

Place the turkey in a preheated 500-degree oven for ½ hour. Set your timer! The intense beginning heat will allow the fat under the skin on the bottom of the turkey (remember—you've got the bird sitting on a rack in the roasting pan) to melt and help brown the skin on the bottom. No more mush-bottomed turkeys! Also, the turkey will begin to turn bronzy brown, which you want. After the initial 500-degree zapping, turn your oven down to a respectable 325 degrees. Do you feel better now?

Follow the timetable on the next page for approximate roasting time. Place a tent of foil loosely over the turkey when it begins to turn golden brown, exposing only the drumsticks to the oven. Roast the turkey until the meat thermometer reads 180 degrees and the juice is no longer pink when you cut into the center of the thigh (it should be clear). The drumstick should move easily in the socket when lifted or twisted. When the turkey is finished roasting, remove it from the oven and let it stand at least ½ hour for easiest carving. However, it's even better to let it rest 1 hour. That way you can count down the rest of the meal. (Timeline to follow.) Keep the turkey tented with foil so it will stay warm.

CHART FOR COOKING YOUR BIRD

The National Turkey Federation recommends you cook your turkey until the temperature reaches 170 degrees in the breast and 180 degrees in the thigh (watch out for the bone). A meat thermometer is distinctly different from a candy thermometer! (I tried to use one for this purpose when I was first learning to cook. It wasn't successful.)

STUFFED TURKEY

8 to 12 pounds	3 to 3½ hours
12 to 14 pounds	3½ to 4 hours
14 to 18 pounds	4 to 4¼ hours
18 to 20 pounds	4¼ to 4¾ hours
20 to 24 pounds	4¾ to 5¼ hours

UNSTUFFED TURKEY

8 to 12 pounds	2¾ hours to 3 hours
12 to 14 pounds	3 to 3¾ hours
14 to 18 pounds	3¾ to 4¼ hours
18 to 20 pounds	4¼ to 4½ hours
20 to 24 pounds	4½ to 5 hours
24 to 30 pounds	5 to 5¼ hours

Right about now, you're probably wondering where the basting instructions are. Personally, I don't baste. Why? Because basting actually dries out the bird! Every time you open the oven door, you lose 25 degrees of heat. And because you lose heat, you have to cook the turkey longer. Longer cooking time means a drier turkey, period. (Yeah, yeah . . . I know you have been basting birds for a hundred years in your family and everyone swears by basting.) I too was in the basting camp till one year I was overwhelmed with all I had to do, and we had the best, juiciest turkey ever. So my advice is: don't baste.

Once the turkey is finished with its roasting, remove it from the oven and let it rest for about 10 minutes in the pan. Then remove your bird from the pan to a cutting board and again, allow it to rest, at least 20 minutes, but 1 hour is better. (And like I said earlier, it gives you a sense of a timetable to finish up the rest of dinner. Just put a little foil jacket on old tom to keep him warm.) This is important because it will retain its juiciness if given the proper "nap."

PAN GRAVY

Let's face it: lumpy gravy just screams amateur. It doesn't take gourmet chef cooking skills to make a lumpless gravy, nor is it rocket science. But for all the mixing, whisking, and fussing, good gravy is a mystery. To do it yourself, you just need a few well-kept secrets. So here you have them, once and for all: gravy demystified.

Here are the ingredients you will need to make gorgeous gravy:

½ carrot
1 celery stalk
½ large onion, quartered
Turkey broth (recipe of sorts; keep reading)
Wondra or Pillsbury flour in a large shaker (yes, buy this)
Salt and pepper to taste
White pepper
Water (as/if needed)

Remember, I promised you I would tell you what to do with the giblet pouch? Now is the time. In that drippy bag you are going to find a big old turkey neck, the heart, gizzard, and liver. The heart, gizzard, and liver are great treats for the dog, but unless giblet gravy is your heart's desire (sorry, couldn't help myself), in my opinion they have no place in a gravy boat.

First, throw the turkey neck, half a carrot, celery stalk, and half an onion, quartered, into a medium saucepan and fill about three-quarters of the way up with cold water. Put the pan on a medium-high heat, bring to a boil, then lower the temp and allow to simmer for about 1 hour or so. Throw a lid on the top and turn it down even lower and allow it to cook for another hour. Strain the broth from the solids (toss the solids) and set aside for later gravy making. If it is hours away from that event, refrigerate the broth.

HITTING THE GRAVY TRAIN

Okay, the turkey has been removed from the pan and is resting comfortably. Skim the big greasy globs of fat from the roasting pan and place in a medium saucepan (there should be about 3 tablespoons or so of fat, depending on the size of your bird). Next, take an equal amount of Wondra flour and add to that turkey grease. (I know this sounds yucky, but you have to trust me.) The heat should be about medium high and you need to whisk away to your heart's content until the roux (pronounced *ROO*) is golden and thick, and naturally lumpless. This roux procedure will take you all of 5 minutes—very easy, you can't mess this up. Set your beauteous roux aside.

Now, back to the roasting pan. Add 1 cup of your reserved turkey stock to the roasting pan and turn up the heat (you will probably need two burners for the job) and bring it to a boil. Using your wire whisk, scrape up all the browned bits off the bottom of the pan. Those browned bits contain concentrated turkey flavor that will make your turkey gravy absolutely to die for. Don't skip this step. Now, add all the golden roux you just made in the saucepan into your roaster, and whisk like your life depended on it. In just moments, a beautiful, velvety bronzed gravy should be emerging and filling you with the joy of accomplishment. Salt and pepper to taste, and add a pinch of white pepper.

I am an admitted snob when it comes to gravy making, but even cookbook authors have their limitations when making enough turkey gravy. Truth be told, a turkey doesn't make as much gravy as necessary for the gravy hounds undoubtedly sitting at your very holiday table. You know the types—they use three ladles of gravy on their potatoes alone, before tackling the turkey on their plates. It is because of them that I came up with this trick. Actually, I take that back. My sister did this and I was shocked at how good it was. I didn't know she had done it at the time or I probably would have thrown myself prostrate on the stove, begging her not to ruin the gravy. Here's what she did: she added a package of dry turkey gravy mix (and the accompanying water) to her already-made gravy. No one was the wiser, including me! I was amazed at how much gravy she had and was thrilled that I (an admitted gravy hound myself) was able to amply ladle gravy without being scolded about "saving some for the next guy." She told me about the sneaky gravy-extension trick after I had polished off Round One of The Meal and noticed there was still gravy left. I nearly needed smelling salts when she told me what she had done. I tried this trick at home and it is simply fabulous. This kind of mix stuff I will do on special occasions, but I will never admit to it, so don't tell a soul you heard this from me.

MUZZIE'S FABULOUS STUFFING

Muzzie is my mom, affectionately nicknamed (it means "confused"—I promise, I only found that out because I like crossword puzzles) by yours truly when I was a smart-mouthed kid. It stuck and now the whole world calls her Muzzie (although some just call her plain Muzz). Muzzie is a great cook, and for many years I tried different gourmet recipes for stuffing, all homemade, none with a mix, but none ever came out better than my mom's. Could be for sentimental reasons, but she definitely has a fan club at my house when it comes to stuffing!

> 1 pound bulk breakfast sausage
> 1½ tablespoons butter, plus a splash of vegetable oil to keep the butter from burning
> 1 large onion, chopped
> 2 celery stalks, chopped
> 1 box (2 envelopes) Mrs. Cubbison's Bread Stuff Mix (on the East Coast, use Pepperidge Farm—not the cornbread kind)
> 1 good handful parsley, finely chopped
> 1 teaspoon poultry seasoning
> 1 (14.75-ounce) can chicken broth (as needed—you won't use the whole thing)

First, cook the sausage in a skillet with about 1 inch of water, over a medium-high heat. You won't be frying it—you'll be poaching it. Use a potato masher to mash the sausage into smallish pieces. You want it thoroughly cooked and not browned and greasy, and not into tiny bits, either. Keep half the remaining water; throw out the rest. Put the cooked sausage and reserved sausage water in a large bowl and set aside—you need to use the skillet again.

Now in that same skillet, heat the butter and oil together over medium-high heat. Add the onion and celery and cook till nice and soft, about 8 minutes.

To the sausage in the bowl, add the sautéed veggies and remaining ingredients *except* the chicken broth. Toss everything together and add a little chicken broth, a bit at a time, to get a soft texture. You will use about ¼ cup of broth or maybe a little more, depending on how dry your dressing is. You want it moist, not drenched. Definitely don't soak the dressing with chicken broth. Save any remaining broth for the gravy.

Place the dressing in a lightly greased casserole dish to be baked later (in a 325 degree oven, covered for about 1 hour; see the timeline for timing). You will bake the dressing an hour before showtime.

ORANGE CRANBERRY SAUCE

Serves 12 (with leftovers)

4 cups (1-pound bag) fresh or frozen cranberries
1 cup water
1½ cups sugar
1 cup orange juice

Rinse the cranberries (even if they are frozen) in a strainer with cool water, and remove any stems and bad or blemished berries.

In a large saucepan, over medium heat, heat the water, sugar, and juice to boiling, stirring occasionally. Continue boiling 5 minutes longer to ensure sugar is completely dissolved, stirring occasionally.

Add the cranberries. Heat over medium heat until boiling again, stirring occasionally. Put a lid on the saucepan, turn down the heat, and simmer about 5 minutes longer, still stirring occasionally, until you hear the cranberries begin to pop. Remove the saucepan from the heat, give it a good stir, and allow mixture to cool for about 20 minutes. Pour the cranberry sauce into a bowl or container and allow to cool completely before refrigerating.

OLD-FASHIONED MASHED POTATOES

Serves 12

12 russet potatoes, peeled and quartered
Unsalted butter
Salt and pepper to taste
Milk

Fill a large pot with water, and as you prepare the potatoes, throw them into the pot after quartering them. After you are finished, drain the water if it looks dirty or murky, and fill it with fresh water. You need to adequately cover the potatoes, but there should be at least a couple of inches of boiling room.

Place the pot of potatoes on a burner, turn heat up to high, and get the potatoes boiling. You can put a lid on it (it will boil faster), but stay in the room so it doesn't boil over. When it starts to boil, bring the heat down to a simmer and cook until fork-tender, about 20 minutes or so, depending on how big your potato quarters are.

Now carefully drain that heavy pot. See if you can draft a big burly guy to do it for you. If not, please be careful!

To your steaming pot of potatoes, add the butter. How much? Well, I don't want to be quoted on how much I use on Thanksgiving (hey, it's a special occasion!); let your conscience be your guide.

Next, add salt and pepper to taste and about ½ cup milk. That's a starting place. Now pull out your potato masher and put some elbow grease into it, or get the big burly guy to do it. *Don't* use the electric mixer on these gems! Potatoes have starch in them, and when you over handle them (as in whip the daylights out of them with an electric mixer), the starch develops, making your lovely mashed potatoes look more like wallpaper paste that needs thinning. Don't go there! Use an old-fashioned potato masher or potato ricer (same kind of deal, only there are little holes in the bottom instead of the usual zigzag pattern of the normal potato masher).

FlyLady does her potatoes earlier in the day and puts them in a Crock-Pot on low heat with a little butter on top to keep them from drying out (and the lid on, too, of course). I think that is ingenious. However, one word of caution: Crock-Pots vary with brand, so you need to make sure yours will work for this task and that the low setting isn't too high. My old one works for this job; my new one is too hot. See what I mean? Test-run a small batch first if you are able.

OVEN-ROASTED SWEET POTATOES AND ONIONS

Serves 12

8 medium sweet potatoes, peeled and cut into 2-inch pieces
4 medium red onions, cut into 1-inch pieces
4 tablespoons extra-virgin olive oil
2 teaspoons lemon pepper
1 teaspoon salt

Preheat the oven to 425 degrees.

Combine all the ingredients in a 9 × 13-inch baking dish. Toss to coat the vegetables with the oil and seasonings, and bake for 35 minutes or so, until the taters are fork-tender and nicely browned.

SAUTÉED GREEN BEANS
WITH NUTMEG

Serves 12

12 handfuls green beans
2 tablespoons butter (I use unsalted)
Splash of olive oil
Salt and pepper to taste
Generous dash of nutmeg (or you can grate it fresh; I have a grater
and it's awesome!)

When you go to the grocery store, count out by the handful how many beans you will need. Give each adult one handful, and count one handful per two small children. Yes, use your hands: grab a handful of beans, plop it into a plastic bag, and consider it a serving.

I know . . . that doesn't give you pounds. Well, it's the best way I know to give you a good idea of what to buy. Who cares if there isn't a weight? (It's probably close to 2½ pounds anyway, if you're cooking for 12.) Here's what you do with those beans:

Wash the beans and string them (pull the string starting at the stem end and pull to the tip). Then snap them in half (or cut them, or leave them whole if they're thin and small). Steam them in a veggie steamer or boil them in a skillet half full of water. When they turn bright green, they're finished. (They will still be a little undercooked.) Strain them and set aside.

In a skillet, heat the butter and oil over medium-high heat and add the well-drained beans. Add the salt and pepper and sauté the beans for 2 to 3 minutes. Add the nutmeg and sauté another minute or so. The beans should be tender, but not mushy.

ROLLS AND BUTTER

Buy the rolls! Buy them from a good bakery or use the frozen dough kind. Make sure they're of a good quality. And buy *butter*, not margarine. I use unsalted, but get whichever you prefer.

PUMPKIN CHEESECAKE

1¼ cups ginger snap crumbs (crush about 20 cookies in a plastic
   bag with a rolling pin)
¼ cup unsalted butter, melted
3 (8-ounce) packages cream cheese, softened
1 cup plus 2 teaspoons sugar
1 teaspoon ground cinnamon
1 teaspoon ground ginger
1 (16-ounce) can pumpkin puree (not pumpkin pie filling)
4 eggs
¾ cup whipping cream, chilled
1 teaspoon vanilla extract

Preheat the oven to 350 degrees.

In a large mixing bowl, mix the crumbs and butter. Press evenly on the bottom of a 9-inch springform pan. Bake 10 minutes, then let cool.

Reduce the oven temperature to 300 degrees.

In another large bowl, beat the cream cheese, 1 cup sugar, the cinnamon, and ginger on medium speed until smooth. Add the pumpkin puree. Now add in the eggs, one at a time, on low speed. Pour the mixture into the springform pan.

Bake until the center is firm, about 1¼ hours. Cool to room temperature. Cover and refrigerate at least 3 hours. (But in your case, you did it two days prior, at least.)

To loosen the cheesecake from the sides of the pan, run a sharp knife between the sides of the pan and the cheesecake, then unbuckle the side and carefully remove. Whip the cream with the remaining sugar and the vanilla until you have soft peaks. Serve a dollop of whipped cream on each serving of the cheesecake.

This recipe is to die for!

Turkey 101

It helps to think of your turkey as just a great big chicken. That brings the intimidation factor down a few notches. During the holiday season, everyone from TV chefs to magazines can tell you how to make the "best turkey ever." This includes tips like brining a turkey, flipping a hot 22-pound turkey mid-roast, or deep-frying it outside using asbestos gloves and safety goggles. Does all of this have you breathing into a paper bag to avoid a panic attack?

Calm down—help is here. If you are a mere mortal who just wants to prepare a decent turkey without all the specialized paraphernalia and techniques, this section is for you.

First, the turkey itself. Should you buy fresh or frozen? Fresh is always a good thing, and the bird is usually more juicy. However, who can resist those deals where you get a free turkey for buying the rest of your groceries at the supermarket, or if you have been given one from the company you work for? Also, frozen turkeys are less expensive.

Personally, I prefer fresh over frozen. You can see the true plumpness of the bird (hard to tell when it's as hard as a cement block) and see the color, too. You want a creamy-skinned bird with smooth skin. Look for any leftover pinfeathers. You can easily pull those out with a pair of tweezers. Also, my preference is a hen over a tom (tom turkeys are bigger, though). I happen to think a hen is more flavorful and tender, although I couldn't find any facts to back that up. So do what works for you—both can produce a tasty bird.

To thaw a frozen turkey, you need adequate time. The turkey should be thawed in your fridge and these big birds take quite a while to thaw completely. Don't try thawing it the night before! You need 24 hours for every 4 to 5 pounds, so if you have a 12-pound bird, it will take about two and a half days to thaw in the fridge. A quick-thaw method is to put the turkey (in its original, sealed plastic wrap) in a sink full of cold water. You will need to change the water every ½ hour or so till thawed. This method will take 6 to 9 hours, depending on the size of your bird.

TURKEY TRIAGE

Got a problem that needs fixing? Here, you find some quick fixes, patches, and helps to pull your dinner from disaster. Gravy too thin? Got lumpy gravy? Turkey taking too long to cook? Stuffing too dry? Cranberries too runny? I have some quick rescues and resuscitations in this section.

WHEN YOU WISH UPON A . . . BONE?

Legend had it that merely touching a wishbone would bring good luck. Naturally, horrible fights and quarrels over who got the wishbone finally brought about the current rite of turkey passage: two people pull on the wishbone until it snaps and the one with the bigger piece of bone gets his or her wish.

When the colonists were first introduced to cranberries by the Indians, they named it a "crane-berry" because the flowers of the berry bent the stalk over, resembling a heron that they called a crane. Cranberries are grown in bogs in New England. Interestingly, before the berries are bagged to be sent to the rest of the country right before Thanksgiving, each berry is bounced at least 4 inches high to make sure it's not too ripe. Who knew?

- Dry stuffing? Melt some butter and add half again as much chicken broth. Heat together and toss in the stuffing. Fluff stuffing with a fork and serve.

- Thin gravy? You need to thicken it with a little more flour. I always use a jar and a lid to minimize the lump factor. Add 1 tablespoon flour to 3 tablespoons *cold* water. Put the lid on and shake violently until you feel your teeth knocking around in your head. (You don't have to shake that hard; I'm trying to make a point.) Add the flour-and-water mixture to the pan of boiling gravy and whisk away as you add it. The gravy will thicken in a matter of moments—just keep whisking!

- Lumpy gravy? You violated the first rule of gravy making: make sure your roux is smooth and lumpless. Gravy making tips are included in the gravy recipe, but suppose you didn't read it and now you have this lumpy mess? Get out the blender and blend the daylights out of this stuff, a *batch* at a time! Fill the blender only half full or you will end up with a turkey-gravy ceiling (you don't want to hear how I know this). Return the gravy to the pan for a quick reheat and voilà! Lumpless gravy!

- Runny cranberries? Pour off some of the juice and call it a day. You could go to all the trouble of trying to thicken the sauce by cooking it some more. (The mixture will thicken naturally because of the pectin in the cranberries, and pectin is released as the cranberries cook.) So the reason your cranberries are runny is that you didn't cook them long enough. I say pull out the strainer, drain off some of the juice, and slap the sauce into a serving dish. Don't you have enough going on without having to redo the cranberries?

- Turkey taking forever to cook? You're probably opening the oven too much, basting it. I did this one year and we ate at about 7 P.M. (planned on eating at 4:00!). Every time you open the oven, you lose about 25 degrees, so shut the oven, raise the temperature about 25 degrees for the next hour (don't baste!), and you should be back on track.

The Timeline

Remember: this is a holiday for *everyone*, including the cook.

TWO WEEKS TO TEN DAYS AHEAD

Order your turkey if you're doing a fresh one. How much turkey will you need? Figure about 1 pound per adult and ½ pound per child, so if you are having 10 adults and 10 children, you will need at least a 15-pound turkey. That will give you what you need, but no leftovers. My philosophy is to buy a big one and enjoy the leftovers!

Firm up your guest list. Call and confirm as necessary.

Although the shopping list is done for you, go through it, double-check what you already have, and head for the market. Yes, buy *everything* now, except the fresh green beans, celery, and parsley (and obviously, the fresh turkey if you ordered one). The only other exception would be the dinner rolls if you're getting them fresh from a bakery. When you buy the cranberries, put them right into the freezer, in the bag they came in, or wait and buy them when you get the green beans and other produce. It's your choice, but I buy them now because I've had a problem getting them (the stores have run out) when it's closer to T-day. The same goes for heavy cream.

When you go shopping, make it easy on yourself. If at all possible, shop during the off hours, without children, and when you are not hungry or having to go to the potty! I am serious . . . you have work to do there, girl!

Plan the table. Are you using linens? Do they need pressing? Press them now and hang them or fold them for later. Nothing is worse than starching a tablecloth just before your guests are due to arrive (ask me how I know this!).

Double-check your serving pieces and serving utensils against the menu. Do you have all the serving pieces you need? Make arrangements now to get or borrow what you don't have. *Don't* do it the day of your dinner! If your great-aunt forgets to bring her gravy boat and ladle, you're up a creek without a paddle (or a ladle, in this case).

ONE WEEK AHEAD

If you have shopped already (and you should have if you're using my plan), make a quick double-check of your list and menu to make sure everything is ready. Take a hint from Santa: make your list and check it twice. This is not the time to forget anything! If you're using my recipes and grocery list, the whole thing is already done for you, so you can skip this step and go have a cup of tea instead. (Isn't this fun?)

Clean out your refrigerator. Be ruthless. You're going to need the room! You may also want to haul out the big cooler from the garage and clean it out to use on T-Day if you're desperate for space. Ask one of your guests to bring ice—you won't have room in your poor beleaguered fridge.

THREE DAYS AHEAD

Pull together all the pieces you are going to use for serving. It is helpful to decide what is going to go in what and write it on a 3 × 5 card, then toss the card into the serving piece. A friend and mentor from my early-married days, Carolyn Dunn, taught me this nifty trick, and it's saved my biscuits more than once. Then, you can stack your bowls, platters, and other serving pieces in one area with the cards in them. Inevitably, on the big day, you will have volunteers in the kitchen just before the time you're ready to serve. Having those cards in place will save your sanity while you're finishing the gravy and getting the bird carved; you can keep the discussion about what goes in where to a minimum because the guesswork is gone.

To keep your serving pieces dust free, cover them with a clean sheet folded in half. Marla Cilley, the FlyLady, even sets her table a few days ahead and puts a clean sheet over the top. When I had a dining room I did the same thing, but now I have only the one table and I use it every day. So use whichever method works for you—just get your serving pieces ready.

Purchase any last-minute fresh items, like the produce mentioned above.

Don't forget: thaw your frozen bird starting today! See "Turkey 101" for more information on thawing a turkey.

TWO DAYS BEFORE

Make the Pumpkin Cheesecake (page 22). When it has completely cooled, cover it with plastic wrap and place in the fridge.

Make the Orange Cranberry Sauce (page 16). Let it completely cool before refrigerating, then cover the sauce with plastic wrap, setting the wrap directly on the sauce. This will keep the sauce from developing a skin.

THE DAY BEFORE

If you ordered a fresh turkey, today's the day to pick it up.

Chop everything and individually bag it in zipper-topped plastic bags: onions and celery for the dressing, veggies for side dishes, and so on. Refrigerate after prepping. Don't do the potatoes or sweet potatoes, though—they'll discolor.

If you haven't done so already, set the table and cover it with a sheet to keep the dust off.

Go over your plan for T-Day and make sure your ducks (turkeys?) are in a row. Double-check everything—your serving pieces, your menu, your guest list, the whole shebang. Determine the time your turkey should go in the oven based on when you want dinner served (don't forget to include your turkey's rest time!). Use the T-Day Countdown list on the next page to help execute the big day. Having that list handy will clear your brain so you can be pleasant with your guests!

Go to bed early! Tomorrow's a big day.

T-Day Countdown

IN THE MORNING

Prepare Muzzie's Fabulous Stuffing (page 14). Put your bird in the oven at the appropriate time based on the Chart for Cooking Your Bird (page 11) and what time you want to serve dinner. Remember, you need to add 1 hour to that time because the bird needs to rest 1 hour out of the oven before serving. Should things get out of control at any point, call the Butterball turkey hotline, 1-800-BUTTERBALL.

Make the stock for the gravy (included in the Pan Gravy recipe).

Wash, peel, and chunk the potatoes for Old-Fashioned Mashed Potatoes (page 17). Place in a pot with cold water. Set aside—not on the stove, or the pot will become warm and the potatoes will begin to cook; they need to stay cool.

Prepare Oven-Roasted Sweet Potatoes and Onions (page 19) to go in the oven; set aside.

Put the butter, salt, and pepper (if not already there) on the table. Consider two butters and two sets of salt and pepper, one on either end.

Remember, clean as you go—it's so much *easier*! Keep a sink full of hot soapy water, and dump stuff in there as you go. Run the dishwasher and empty it after this little blitz.

Take a time-out and put your feet up. On your way to your favorite chair, double-check the bathroom for clean guest towels, hand soap, and extra toilet paper.

ONE HOUR BEFORE

At this point, your turkey should be finished roasting and resting comfortably. Don't forget to give him his foil jacket so he doesn't get cold. You still have a lot to do; if someone volunteers to help, let the person help!

Cook Muzzie's Fabulous Stuffing (the pan with stuffing that didn't go in the bird if you stuffed).

Cook the Old-Fashioned Mashed Potatoes and place in a Crock-Pot on low. (I strongly urge you to test-drive this to make sure your cooker will not run too hot for this task.)

Cook the Oven-Roasted Sweet Potatoes and Onions. If you have only one oven, you have a temperature conflict with the stuffing. Here's how to handle that. Cook this recipe as is, and place Muzzie's

Fabulous Stuffing (covered with foil) in the oven after your Oven-Roasted Sweet Potatoes and Onions have finished cooking. At this point, there is only 20 minutes left and the stuffing can take the heat as long as it is covered and sealed. When you pull out the sweet potatoes, immediately lower the oven temperature to 350 degrees and finish heating the stuffing (probably less time than the recipe calls for because of the initial blast of higher heat). Be flexible—stuffing is easy as long as you keep it covered so it won't dry out. Keep everything warm after cooking.

Cook the Sautéed Green Beans with Nutmeg (page 20). Keep them warm after cooking.

Carve the turkey. See the step-by-step illustration on page 30 for how to carve a turkey.

Make the Pan Gravy (page 12).

Heat the rolls.

Put the cranberries in the serving dish with a utensil and on the table or buffet.

Whip the cream (or do it later . . . that's what I do).

Set up the coffeemaker so all you have to do is flick the switch.

TIME TO EAT!

Start getting everything in its serving dish: turkey on the platter with a serving utensil; rolls in the basket (or baskets) with the napkin to keep them warm; green beans and sweet potatoes in their serving dishes; gravy in its boat; stuffing or dressing in its dish; and of course, the mashed potatoes in their dish.

You've earned your kudos! Take the compliments, enjoy your family and friends, and most important, give thanks.

Living with Leftovers

The turkey's been gobbled (sorry—couldn't help myself) along with all the trimmings, and now you have this *huge* half-eaten turkey sitting in your fridge. You can eat only so many sandwiches! What are you going to do with it all?

HOW TO CARVE TURKEY

1. Let the turkey rest for an hour before carving, and then remove it from the pan. This will be easier to do if you make two heavy-duty strips of aluminum foil to act as lifters (unless you have turkey lifters).

2. To start carving, first remove the turkey legs. Using the carving fork, hold the bird firmly against the cutting board and slice through the skin between the breast and thigh—there is an obvious gap. Pull back the leg to locate the joint, then cut through the joint to remove the whole leg. Repeat on the other side.

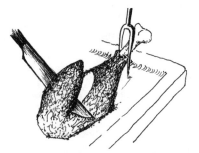

3. You need to separate the thigh from the drumstick. To do this, stretch the thigh and the drumstick apart, find the joint, and with a firm downward movement of the knife, cut all the way through the joint.

4. Unless you have invited Fred Flintstone for Thanksgiving, you're going to want to carve the meat off the drumstick. Place the carving fork on the cutting board and aim the narrow end of the leg between the tines, so you don't pierce the meat. Now slice the meat off the drumstick.

5. You may want to cut the slices from the thigh, working parallel to the bone, as seen in the illustration. You can easily remove the wing using your hand to disjoint it from the breast, or simply cut through, once you have located the joint.

6. Now that you've taken all the appendages off, you need to carve the breast meat. Starting at the outside of the breast, cut the slices diagonally. Do this on both sides of the turkey and ta-da—you've carved the bird!

In my opinion, turkey is the ultimate leftover. It is a continuous feast because out of one meal, you can get at least two more. In the case of turkey, it's probably even more. So here are some incredible recipes to get you using up that turkey and enjoying every mouthful.

BEANLESS TURKEY CHILI

Serves 4

2 tablespoons olive oil
1 large onion, chopped
4 garlic cloves, pressed
1 celery stalk, chopped
1 red bell pepper, seeded, deribbed, and chopped
2 jalapeño peppers, seeded, deribbed, and chopped (optional)
1–2 teaspoons ground cumin
2 teaspoons ground coriander
½ teaspoon cayenne pepper
Salt and pepper to taste
1 (28-ounce) can tomatoes, broken up
4–5 cups chopped cooked turkey (see Note)
2 tablespoons chopped fresh cilantro
Juice of 1 lime

In a large saucepan or skillet, heat the oil over medium heat. Sauté the onion, garlic, celery, peppers, and seasonings over medium-low heat for about 5 minutes.

Add the tomatoes. Simmer gently for 20 minutes. Stir in the turkey and cook until heated through. Before serving, add cilantro and lime juice and stir gently.

SERVING SUGGESTIONS: Serve in bowls and top with shredded Cheddar cheese and blops of sour cream. Serve with a big green salad and cornbread muffins.

NOTE: If you don't have that much turkey left, add 1 drained can of white beans and 1 cup of drained canned corn, and it becomes more of a chili.

BARBECUED TURKEY PASTA

1 pound fusilli or other medium pasta
1 tablespoon olive oil
3 cups cubed leftover turkey
1 small green bell pepper, thinly sliced
1 small red onion, thinly sliced
2 garlic cloves, pressed
½ cup spaghetti sauce
¼ cup barbecue sauce
1 cup grated Provolone cheese
3 green onions, chopped
¼ cup chopped cilantro

Prepare the pasta according to package directions. Meanwhile, heat the oil in a large skillet over medium heat. Add the turkey and sauté, stirring occasionally, until it starts to brown on all sides, about 1 minute. Add the bell pepper, onion, and garlic and cook until pepper turns bright green, about 1 minute. Add your favorite spaghetti sauce and barbecue sauce, and heat just to a simmer. Remove from the heat.

Drain the pasta, reserving ¼ cup cooking water and return pasta to the pot. Add the turkey mixture and cheese to the pot. Stir over low heat until the pasta is coated with sauce. Add enough of the reserved cooking water, if needed, to make the sauce lightly coat the pasta (you don't want it too thin, however). Serve the pasta in bowls and top with green onions and chopped cilantro.

SERVING SUGGESTIONS: A big spinach salad and whole-grain rolls.

HANUKKAH

Hanukkah, also known as the Festival of Lights, has a great story behind the celebration. But even with the thrilling story of how the Jews lived through yet another oppressive time, how the oil for the temple was miraculously extended by God to burn for eight days, my question still is, so why all the fried foods?

My friend Judy Gruen, who also beautifully explained Passover (page 119), is here to elucidate the details:

Don't ask me how this happened, but Hanukkah has become one oily holiday. One of the best-known and most festive holidays on the Jewish calendar, Hanukkah celebrates a miraculous military victory of a tiny band of committed Jews against ancient Greek oppressors. These Greeks tried to force the Jews to assimilate into Greek culture, forsaking all meaningful Jewish religious tradition. After the battle was won, the Jews reentered their war-battered Temple and found only one tiny jar of pure oil with which to light the Temple menorah. Another miracle occurred: these few drops of oil kept the menorah burning brightly for eight days!

Today Hanukkah is celebrated by the lighting of our own menorahs in our windows each night for the eight days of the holiday. And, in a boon for manufacturers of olive and corn oil, we also indulge in fried potato pancakes known as latkes, as well as special Hanukkah doughnuts called sufganiyot. These sufganiyot are usually filled with jelly, cream, or (my favorite) chocolate. How did a victory over Greeks become a capitulation to grease? Who knows? Just be thankful the holiday lasts only a week, and make sure to enjoy. After all, it is a holiday!

Hanukkah Decor

The centerpiece of Hanukkah is, of course, the beautiful menorah set in a place of honor. For each of the eight nights, one additional candle on the menorah is lit, until all eight are burning on the last night. Decorating is kept to a minimum because, according to my friend Judy, "There's too much to do in the kitchen!" That may be so, but this *is* the Festival of Lights. Bring on the rest of your candles and use them. Turn off all the lights and allow your table to be lit with the light of candles only. Imagine the memories you are instilling in your children!

Fine linen tablecloths and napkins should be used for these nightly celebrations, as well as pretty flowers to match your decor. It doesn't take much, though—and like Judy said, you've got much to do in the kitchen!

The Menu

SWEET POTATO LATKES

CROCK-POT APPLESAUCE

CARAWAY CHICKEN

BRAISED RED CABBAGE

EASY BANANA CAKE

JUDY'S SUFGANIYOT

THE SHOPPING LIST

MEAT

3- to 4-pound chicken, cut up

CONDIMENTS

Vegetable oil

Olive oil

Fruit preserves

PRODUCE

Sweet potatoes (enough for 2 cups coarsely grated and well
    packed)

1 small red bell pepper

1 bunch cilantro

1½ pounds Granny Smith apples

1½ pounds Red Delicious apples

2 lemons

Red cabbage (12 cups shredded)

Bananas (1 cup mashed)

CANNED GOODS

1 (15-ounce) can chickpeas

SPICES

Ground cumin

Cinnamon

Caraway seeds

Black peppercorns

Vanilla extract

DAIRY/DAIRY CASE

Eggs (5)

Margarine (pareve)

Soy milk (¼ cup)

DRY GOODS

Cornstarch

Unbleached all-purpose flour

Cake flour

Brown sugar

White sugar

Baking soda

1 (7-ounce) package kosher chocolate chips (optional)

1 package active dry yeast

TOOLS OF THE TRADE

You probably have most of these, but double-check to make sure.

Food processor

Electric mixer

Large Crock-Pot

Mortar and pestle (for a good stand-in, see sidebar on page 40)

2-inch round biscuit cutter

Basting brush

9-inch square baking pan

SWEET POTATO LATKES

Serves 6 (generously)

2 cups (well packed) peeled and coarsely grated sweet potatoes
½ cup chopped red bell pepper
3 tablespoons cornstarch
1 (15-ounce) can chickpeas, drained
1 egg
½ teaspoon ground cumin
Salt and pepper to taste
¼ cup chopped cilantro
½ cup vegetable oil

Preheat the oven to 325 degrees.

In a large mixing bowl, combine the sweet potatoes and bell pepper. Add the cornstarch, tossing to coat.

Meanwhile, in a food processor, puree the chickpeas to a coarse paste. Add the egg, cumin, and salt and pepper, blending well. Transfer the chickpea mixture to a small bowl. Mix in the cilantro, then add all of this to the sweet potato mixture, mixing thoroughly.

In a large skillet, heat 6 tablespoons oil over medium-high heat. Working in batches, drop 1 heaping tablespoon of batter per latke into the hot oil. Using the back of your spoon, spread the little latke blobs into 3-inch rounds. Cook until nicely browned, about 3 minutes per side. (The remaining 2 tablespoons oil are there in case you need them to cook more latkes.) As your latkes are finished cooking, place them on a paper towel–lined plate.

Transfer the cooked latkes to a baking sheet and place in the oven to keep warm until serving.

CROCK-POT APPLESAUCE

Serves 6 (or more)

Meet two of my fa-
vorite relatives—the mor-
tar and pestle. It's a dual
tool that no home cook
should be without. It will
coarsely grind peppercorns
and any other seeds you
need roughly ground for
recipes such as the Car-
away Chicken (page 41).
But what if you don't have
one of these handy-dandy
kitchen tools?

Use a coffee cup (not a
fine china one, but one that
is thick and heavy) and the
bottom of a glass spice
bottle for an improvised
contraption that is nearly
as good as the real deal.
Put the item to be ground
in the bottom of the cup
and use the glass spice jar
(cleaned, of course) to
grind it. Go easy and your
results will be top-notch.

*3 pounds apples, cored, peeled, and cut into chunks (any mixture,
   but I like half Granny Smith and half Red Delicious)*
½ cup brown sugar
½ teaspoon cinnamon

Place the apples directly in the Crock-Pot. Toss together with the
brown sugar and cinnamon, then cook on low for 8 hours or so; check
this often—the pot size, age, and so on may make your cooking time
more or less. Your whole house will smell wonderful!

Allow the applesauce to cool, then refrigerate till ready to use.

CARAWAY CHICKEN

Serves 6

2 tablespoons caraway seeds
¼ teaspoon black peppercorns
1 teaspoon finely chopped lemon zest
Salt to taste
1 3- to 4-pound chicken, cut up
2 teaspoons lemon juice
1 lemon, cut in wedges

Preheat the oven to 375 degrees.

With a mortar and pestle, slightly crush the caraway seeds and peppercorns. Stir in the lemon zest and salt (see sidebar page 113, How to Zest a Lemon).

Rub the spice mixture over the chicken and under the skin of the breast. Place the chicken in a shallow pan. Roast, uncovered, for about 1 hour or until the meat is no longer pink.

Drizzle the lemon juice over the chicken before serving and serve with additional lemon wedges.

BRAISED RED CABBAGE

Serves 6

12 cups shredded red cabbage
6 tablespoons olive oil
Salt and pepper to taste
Water

In a very large skillet with a tight-fitting lid (or if you don't have a skillet large enough to handle all 12 cups of cabbage, then batch it, divvying up the olive oil accordingly), heat the olive oil over medium-high heat. Add the cabbage and sauté, salt and peppering as you go. When you have sautéed for about 2 or 3 minutes, it's time to add a little water (about ½ inch of water) and get the lid on the pan. Reduce the heat to medium-low and allow the cabbage to cook till tender, about 5 minutes or so depending on the thickness of your cabbage shreds. Keep an eye on your cabbage and, if necessary, add a little more water.

Remove from the pan and place in a serving bowl.

EASY BANANA CAKE

Serves 6–8

½ cup margarine (pareve)

1¼ cups sugar

2 eggs, beaten

¼ cup soy milk

1 teaspoon vanilla extract

1 teaspoon baking soda

1 cup mashed banana—smooth, no lumps

1½ cups cake flour

Preheat the oven to 350 degrees. Lightly grease and flour a 9-inch square baking pan.

In a large bowl, using electric beaters, cream the margarine and sugar until light and fluffy. Add the eggs and beat some more. In a small bowl, combine the soy milk and vanilla, then dissolve baking soda in it. Add the soy milk mixture to the margarine mixture, blending well. Now add the mashed banana and mix in. Add the cake flour and mix well.

Pour the batter into your prepared pan and bake for 45 minutes, or until cake is done. Test by inserting a toothpick in the middle and pulling out. If it's clean, the cake is done.

LET THEM EAT CAKE

Cake flour is a decidedly different flour from all-purpose flour, or most any other flour you can name off the top of your head. Cake flour's whole purpose is to produce light and airy baked goods by being lower in gluten than most off-the-shelf flours. The opposite of cake flour is bread flour, which has a higher gluten content (that's good for bread, bad for cakes).

If cake flour is unavailable at your market, see if you can find pastry flour, which is about the same thing (although cake flour supposedly has a higher gluten content). I have had remarkably good results using whole wheat pastry flour for regular cake flour. One thing that bugs me about cake flour, besides the fact that it's white flour, is that it's *bleached* white flour and is absolutely null and void of anything even closely resembling nutrients. Though these are celebratory foods, I still like to sneak a little nutrition into the menu.

JUDY'S SUFGANIYOT

Serves 6

This recipe needs to be started the night before.

> 1 package active dry yeast
> 4 tablespoons sugar
> ¾ cup lukewarm water
> 2½ cups unbleached all-purpose flour
> Pinch of salt
> 1 teaspoon cinnamon
> 2 eggs, separated
> 2 tablespoons margarine (pareve)
> Fruit preserves and/or kosher chocolate chips
> Vegetable oil, for frying
> Sugar

In a large bowl, mix the yeast, half the sugar, and the warm water. Let the yeast proof; it will bubble up in the bowl.

In another bowl, sift the flour. Re-measure to the proper amount (flour will invariably measure out with more after sifting), then mix the sifted flour with the remaining sugar, salt, cinnamon, egg yolks, and margarine. Gradually add the yeast mixture to the flour, stirring well to incorporate. Cover the egg whites with plastic wrap and refrigerate for tomorrow.

Take the dough out of the bowl and plop it on a counter sprinkled with a little flour. Knead the dough until it forms a nice ball. Cover your dough with a towel and let it rise overnight in the refrigerator.

The next day, sprinkle your countertop again with flour and roll out the dough to a thickness of about ⅛ inch.

Cut the dough into 24 rounds with a 2-inch round biscuit cutter. Take ½ teaspoon of preserves (or if you want chocolate, about 6 chocolate chips should do the trick) and place in the center of half the rounds. Top with the remaining rounds. Press down the edges carefully using your fingers, then brush with egg white to seal. Let them rise for about 30 minutes.

In a large skillet, heat about 2 inches of oil over medium-high heat. Your oil needs to get to approximately 375 degrees. To test if the temperature is right, drop a little scrap of dough in the oil. The scrap should float on the top and brown quickly. If your oil is smoking, it's too hot; if the scrap isn't cooking fast enough, it's too cold.

Once the oil is the right temperature, drop the doughnuts into the hot oil, about four or five at a time for about 5 minutes on each side, or until golden brown on both sides. Drain well on paper towels, then roll in sugar and serve.

The Timeline

TEN DAYS AHEAD

Plan the table. If using linens, do they need pressing? Press them now and hang them or fold them for later.

Double-check your serving pieces and utensils and equipment against your menu. Make arrangements *now* to buy or borrow anything you need.

THREE DAYS AHEAD

Clean out your refrigerator. Take your shopping list to the grocery store and buy everything.

ONE DAY AHEAD

Pull out all the pieces you are going to use for serving and write the name of the item that is going to be served in that bowl or platter on a 3 × 5 card. Place it on the serving piece. You can then stack your bowls, platters, and other serving pieces in one area with the cards already in them. This will save any confusion at serving time. Cover these items with a clean sheet or towel to keep them dust free.

THE NIGHT BEFORE

Prepare dough for Judy's Sufganiyot (page 44), and refrigerate. Set the table and cover it with a sheet to keep the dust off. Double-check everything—serving pieces, menu, and so on.

CHRISTMAS

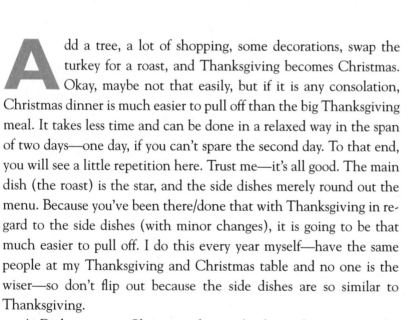

Add a tree, a lot of shopping, some decorations, swap the turkey for a roast, and Thanksgiving becomes Christmas. Okay, maybe not that easily, but if it is any consolation, Christmas dinner is much easier to pull off than the big Thanksgiving meal. It takes less time and can be done in a relaxed way in the span of two days—one day, if you can't spare the second day. To that end, you will see a little repetition here. Trust me—it's all good. The main dish (the roast) is the star, and the side dishes merely round out the menu. Because you've been there/done that with Thanksgiving in regard to the side dishes (with minor changes), it is going to be that much easier to pull off. I do this every year myself—have the same people at my Thanksgiving and Christmas table and no one is the wiser—so don't flip out because the side dishes are so similar to Thanksgiving.

A Dickens-esque Christmas dinner (without the goose or the ghost) can be done without too much fuss and worry. It's as simple as following the directions below. Really! You can do this.

The Menu

ROAST BEAST (THIS IS WHAT MY KIDS CALL IT; IT IS
  ROAST BEEF, ACTUALLY)

CREAMED HORSERADISH

PAN GRAVY

OLD-FASHIONED MASHED POTATOES

ROASTED BUTTERNUT SQUASH AND ONIONS

SAUTÉED GREEN BEANS WITH NUTMEG (SAME AS
  THANKSGIVING. WHY MESS WITH A GOOD THING?)

ROLLS AND BUTTER

EASY TRIFLE

CRÈME ANGLAIS

THE SHOPPING LIST

MEAT

3-pound rump roast (and a little extra beef fat)

1 pound beef short ribs

CONDIMENTS

1 jar prepared horseradish

Extra-virgin olive oil

1 (4-ounce) jar seedless raspberry jam (or seeded, if
  seedless is not available)

Cream sherry (optional)

PRODUCE

6 handfuls green beans

2 medium red onions

3 pounds onions (keep these on hand for regular cooking
  anyway)

1 bunch carrots

1 bunch celery

1 head garlic

1 butternut squash (I'd go for a bigger one, 2 to 3 pounds)

6 large russet potatoes

1 pint berries (buy what is available and good and affordable)

SPICES

Garlic powder

Nutmeg

Lemon pepper

Vanilla extract

White pepper

DAIRY/DAIRY CASE

1 pint half-and-half (plus extra for the coffee)

Eggs (8)

Unsalted butter (3 tablespoons, plus what you will serve with dinner rolls)

1 pint heavy cream

1 (8-ounce) container sour cream

Milk (½–1 cup)

DRY GOODS

Wondra flour (it's in a blue canister)

Sugar (1 cup)

Coffee

FROZEN FOODS

2 Sara Lee frozen pound cakes

Rolls (if not using bakery rolls)

BAKERY

Rolls

TOOLS OF THE TRADE

The things you may need to borrow or purchase are a meat thermometer (big-time important; buy one if you don't own one) and a trifle bowl or straight-sided salad bowl (clear glass is preferable).

Wire whisk

Roasting pan

Roasting rack

Meat carving set

Meat thermometer

Potato masher

Trifle bowl (or salad bowl with straight sides)

9 × 13-inch baking dish

ROAST BOAST

To make a delectable, wonderful roast beast, you need to take these tips into serious consideration before you start:

- Warm up. To ensure even cooking, you need to make sure your beast has been brought to room temperature (take it out of the fridge about an hour or so before you plan to start roasting). This prevents uneven cooking because there are no cold spots. But that doesn't mean you take a fresh piece of beef out the night before and let it sit on the countertop for 8 hours!

- Rack it up. Your roasting pan should have a rack for the beast to sit on. Invest in a good roasting pan with a properly fitting rack. This investment should set you back a few bucks, but the payoff is the final product. I bought myself a really nice roasting pan last year for Thanksgiving and spent some significant change on it. The resulting best turkey I had ever cooked (and I've cooked a *lot* of turkeys) has me 100 percent convinced: do not skimp on good tools that will last you a lifetime. My roasting pan is highly favored among all my kitchen tools. Remember, too, that the object of roasting is to surround the food with dry heat. When the meat is racked, you are surrounding it, as opposed to having it sit on a pan and get mushy on the bottom and not cook as evenly as it could.

- Fat up. Place the fatty side of the beef up on the rack when you first start roasting. This helps the beast to self-baste.

- Pull it early. Say you need to cook your beast for 2 hours. Pull it from the oven 15 minutes early. It is going to continue cooking during the rest time, so it will be timed just right if you keep this in mind.

The Recipes

ROAST BEAST

Serves 6

I really wanted to do a beef tenderloin one year. Then I found out how much it was a pound! A good rump roast will be just as flavorful as tenderloin, and you won't have to take out a second mortgage on your house.

This is a wonderful, flavorful roast. Make sure you have the butcher give you a little extra fat on the side. You will want some short ribs or other beefy bones to make a gravy with, too.

> *3-pound rump roast*
> *A little extra beef fat*
> *Salt and pepper to taste*
> *Garlic powder to taste*

Preheat the oven to 500 degrees.

Wash the roast and pat dry with paper towels (this is important).

Insert a meat thermometer into the thickest part of the roast, if using a thermometer. Roast on a wire rack in a large roasting pan for 15 minutes, then turn the oven down to a respectable 375 degrees and roast for 1¾ hours, or to desired doneness. For a medium-rare roast, the meat thermometer should read 135 degrees.

Let the roast sit for 10 minutes on the rack. Then remove it to a cutting board to sit for another 10 or 15 minutes. Roasts absolutely need to sit for a little bit, otherwise the meat is flabby and weird. It also cuts better, is more juicy, and has better flavor after it sits.

Cut thin slices and serve with Creamed Horseradish and Pan Gravy. *Yum!!*

WHERE'S THE BEEF?

That was the cry heard 'round the world twenty years ago by a cranky little lady named Clara Peller, who got a tad upset when there wasn't enough ground round between her hamburger's buns. A lot has changed since 1984. Not only is it hip to beef up the protein in your meals, but today's beef is a lot leaner. One thing that has stayed the same is finding the right cut and knowing what to look for.

So let's mooove over to the meat department and take a lesson in choosing a choice piece of beef.

- *Love Me Tender.* Make sure the meat you are purchasing is tender to the touch. If it is rough, that means the animal was either too old or stressed when it was butchered.
- *Glean for Lean.* There are lots of choices out there. Make sure you look for the one piece that isn't too marbled. True, marbling means tender, but it also means *fat*.
- *Old Is Gold.* Aged beef is better because the connective tissue breaks down, yielding a tenderer cut of beef. Look for beef that has been aged at least 14 days.
- *Think Pink.* Or red even, but never brown. Brown meat is a sign that it may be spoiled. Stay clear and go for the pink or red cuts of meat.

CREAMED HORSERADISH

This is absolutely delicious and I offer no recipe. It's all a matter of taste and the amount of "kick" you and your guests can tolerate.

I was raised eating roast beef nearly every Sunday night. My father was British, and we didn't even eat *creamed* horseradish; it was straight horseradish, right from the jar. I learned to love it from an early age.

Consequently, when I discovered the subtlety of creamed horseradish, I still made it relatively strong, using a 1:1 ratio, horseradish to sour cream. Make a little batch of it this way, taste it (with a glass of water handy), and then add more sour cream as necessary.

You need prepared horseradish (Morehouse, French's, and a few others make this—it's just plain, though, and in a jar in the condiment section of the grocery store) and sour cream (8 ounces is more than adequate).

PAN GRAVY

1 pound beef short ribs
2 onions, chopped
6 garlic cloves
3 carrots, snapped in half
2 celery stalks, snapped in half
Olive oil
Salt and pepper to taste
Water (as needed)

Preheat the oven to 400 degrees.

Before you get your roast started, you're going to want to get the bones roasting so you can make a lot of gravy. Place the short ribs in a roasting pan or baking dish. Add the onions, garlic, carrots, and celery. Drizzle olive oil over the top, sprinkle on salt and pepper, and place in the oven for 45 minutes to 1 hour. The bones should be bronzed and browned, and so should the vegetables.

At the end of the cooking time, scrape everything into a soup pot, cover with cold water, and bring to a boil over high heat. Use a wire whisk and water to scrape up any stuck bits off the bottom of the baking pan and add to the pot. Let the pot boil at a fairly rigorous rate uncovered (you can cover it to get it started; it will come to a boil faster that way), and cook for nearly 1 hour. You should get a nice strong, browned liquid at the end of this: this will be gravy later on. Strain the broth and reserve.

At Thanksgiving, we put the kibosh on lumpy gravy. Beautiful gravy is something you can make; you don't have to be Emeril to kick your gravy-making skills up a notch, either. Follow this simple step-by-step guide and watch how your velvety gravy emerges!

Here are the ingredients you will need to make gorgeous gravy.

Reserved beef stock (you just made this with bones)
Wondra or Pillsbury's fine flour (you should have this left over from
*   Thanksgiving)*
Salt and pepper to taste
White pepper

Okay, your roast has been removed from the pan and is resting comfortably. Skim the big greasy globs of fat from the roasting pan and place in a medium saucepan (there should be about 3 tablespoons or so of fat). Next, take an equal amount of Wondra flour and add to the beef grease (I know this sounds gross, but if you trust me with your turkey gravy, you can trust me with your roast beef gravy, too). The heat should be about medium-high, and you need to whisk away to your heart's content until the roux is golden and thick, and naturally lumpless. This roux procedure will take you all of 5 minutes—very easy, you can't mess this up. Set your smooth roux aside.

Now back to the roasting pan. Add a cup of your reserved beef stock to the roasting pan and turn up the heat (you will probably need two burners for the job) and bring it to a boil. Using your wire whisk, scrape up all the browned bits from the bottom of the pan. Those browned bits contain concentrated beef flavor that will make your gravy gourmet quality. Don't skip this step. Now add the golden roux you just made and whisk like your life depended on it, salt and peppering to taste; add just a pinch of white pepper for that extra punch. In just moments, a beautiful, velvety brown gravy should emerge and fill you once again with the joy of accomplishment.

OLD-FASHIONED
MASHED POTATOES

Serves 6

6 russet potatoes, peeled and quartered
Unsalted butter
Salt and pepper to taste
Milk

Fill a large pot with water, and as you prepare the potatoes, throw them into the pot after quartering them. After you are finished, drain the water if it looks dirty or murky, and fill the pot with fresh cold water. You need to adequately cover the potatoes, but there should be at least a couple of inches of cooking room.

Place the pot of potatoes on a burner, turn heat up to high, and get the potatoes boiling. You can put a lid on it (it will boil faster), but stay in the room so it doesn't boil over. When it starts to boil, bring the heat down to a simmer and cook until fork-tender, about 20 minutes or so, depending on how big your potato quarters are.

Now carefully drain that heavy pot. See if you can draft a big burly guy to do it for you. If not, please be careful!

To your steaming pot of potatoes, add the butter. How much? Well, I don't want to be quoted on how much I use on Christmas (hey, it's a special occasion!); let your conscience be your guide.

Next, add salt and pepper to taste and add about ½ cup milk. That's a starting place. Now pull out your potato masher and put some elbow grease into it, or get the big burly guy to do it. *Don't* use the electric mixer on these gems! Potatoes have gluten in them, and when you overhandle them (as in whip the daylights out of them with an electric mixer), the gluten develops, making your lovely mashed potatoes look more like wallpaper paste that needs thinning. Don't go there! Use an old-fashioned potato masher or potato ricer (same kind of deal, only there are little holes in the bottom instead of the usual zigzag pattern of the normal potato masher).

ROASTED BUTTERNUT SQUASH AND ONIONS

Serves 6

Can be made a day ahead and heated up later

1 large butternut squash, peeled and cut into 2-inch cubes
2 medium red onions, cut into 1-inch pieces
1–2 tablespoons extra-virgin olive oil
2 teaspoons lemon pepper
1 teaspoon salt

Preheat the oven to 425 degrees.

Combine all the ingredients in a 9 × 13-inch baking dish. Toss to coat vegetables with oil and seasonings, and bake for 35 minutes or so, until the butternut is fork-tender and nicely browned.

SAUTÉED GREEN BEANS WITH NUTMEG

Serves 6

6 handfuls green beans
1 tablespoon butter (I use unsalted)
Splash of olive oil
Salt and pepper to taste
Generous dash of nutmeg (or you can grate it fresh, I have a grater and it's awesome!)

When you go to the grocery store, count out by the handful how many beans you will need. Give each adult one handful, and count one handful per two small children. Yes, use your hands: grab a handful of beans, plop it into a plastic bag, and consider it a serving.

I know . . . that doesn't give you pounds. It's the best way I know to give you a good idea of what to buy. Who cares if there isn't a weight? (It's probably close to 1¼ pounds anyway, if you're cooking for 6.)

Here's what you do with those beans:

Wash the beans and string them (pull the string starting at the stem end and pull to the tip). Then snap them in half (or cut them, or leave them whole if they're thin and small). Steam them in a veggie steamer or boil them in a skillet half full of water. When they turn bright green, they're finished. (They will still be a little undercooked.) Strain them and set aside.

In a skillet, heat the butter and oil over medium-high heat and add the well-drained beans. Add the salt and pepper and sauté the beans for about 2 to 3 minutes. Add a touch of nutmeg and sauté another minute or so. The beans should be tender, but not mushy.

ROLLS AND BUTTER

Buy the rolls! Buy them from a good bakery or use the frozen dough kind. Make sure they're of a good quality. And buy *butter*, not margarine.

EASY TRIFLE

Serves 6 (or more)

My dad was quite the cook, and he often made his English trifle, which was traditional, but it floated in entirely too much sherry and a liquidy custard. I didn't like it because it was so soggy and boozy. In my young mind, eating trifle was equivalent to eating something that had a cocktail accidentally spilled on it—and who wants to eat accidental cuisine? So I came up with my own version that not only preserves the integrity of the pound cake but also gives those who don't want the sherry some options. Trust me, this is easy, fabulous, and you are going to love it.

> *2 Sara Lee frozen pound cakes, thawed and sliced*
> *1 (4-ounce) jar raspberry preserves (I prefer the seedless)*
> *1 pint whipping cream (not Cool Whip and not the stuff in a can)*
> *1 pint fresh raspberries (or whatever other berry you can find fresh, or skip)*
> Crème Anglais (page 62)
> Cream sherry (optional)

In a footed trifle bowl (or a salad bowl with straight sides), layer everything, starting with pound cake slices spread with a generous spoonful of raspberry preserves on top. Place the first layer on the bottom with the jam side up.

Then add a layer of whipped cream, then some berries, then more pound cake smeared with raspberry jam. Do it again. End with whipped cream on top. Garnish with any remaining berries.

Serve with Crème Anglais, and the sherry on the side in a pitcher.

CRÈME ANGLAIS

This is easy to make, but you must follow the directions exactly. You don't want the half-and-half to boil! It will break and you will have scrambled eggs floating in your sauce. Not good. For those in the UK and Australia, half-and-half is half cream and half milk.

> 2 cups half-and-half
> 1 cup sugar
> 2½ teaspoons vanilla extract
> 8 egg yolks
> 4 tablespoons unsalted butter

In a saucepan over medium heat, combine the half-and-half, half the sugar, and 2 teaspoons vanilla.

In a medium bowl, whisk together the egg yolks and remaining sugar until smooth.

When the cream mixture starts to just come to a boil, remove it from the heat. Whisk a small amount of hot cream into the egg yolk mixture, then pour the egg yolk mixture into the remaining hot cream and whisk until smooth.

Return it to the heat and cook over medium heat, stirring, until mixture coats the back of a metal spoon and is slightly thickened. Remove from heat and stir in the butter and remaining vanilla. To keep it from getting a skin on top, put plastic wrap directly on the surface.

Christmas Dinner Rescue

So there you are, standing over a pan of thin or lumpy gravy, overcooked meat, and horseradish sauce that makes your eyes water! Here's how to fix those messes:

- Thin gravy? You need to thicken it with a little more flour. I always use a jar with a lid to minimize the lump factor. Add 1 tablespoon of flour to 3 tablespoons *cold* water, put the lid on, and shake violently until you feel your teeth knocking around in your head. (You don't have to shake that hard; I'm trying to make a point.) Add the flour and water mixture to the pan of boiling gravy and whisk away as you add it. The gravy will thicken in a matter of moments—just keep whisking!

- Lumpy gravy? You violated the first rule of gravy making: make sure your roux is smooth and lumpless. Gravy-making tips are included in "Hitting the Gravy Train" on page 12 in the Thanksgiving section, but suppose you didn't read it and now you have this lumpy mess? Get out the blender and blend the daylights out of this stuff, a *batch* at a time! Only fill the blender *half* full or you will end up with a thoroughly gravied ceiling (this is called learning your lesson the hard way). Return the gravy back to the pan for a quick reheating and voilà! Lumpless gravy!

- Overcooked your beast? First, remove any blackened edges with a knife and serve with an abundance of gravy over the top. Skip the platter and serve directly to the individual dinner plates. Put the extra gravy in a boat on the table, however. Garnish the gravied meat with chopped parsley. Remember: chopped parsley hides a multitude of sins.

- Horseradish sauce making your eyes tear up? Add more sour cream. Out of sour cream? Add anything dairy—a little milk, a little cream cheese (thinned out with some milk), even a little plain yogurt. Dairy binds to the "hot" stuff and helps tame the savage heat.

Just for Fun: Fruitcake as a *Gift?*

No one ever got fat from fruitcake. That is a fact. Fruitcake is one of those indestructible things that even nuclear fallout won't harm. Only fruitcake and cockroaches can make that claim. All that candied fruit, nuts, and brandy, or whatever flammable liquid one soaks them in, could easily be used commercially to detonate condemned buildings or be sold for billions of dollars to NASA to fuel rockets.

Whoever thought up fruitcake, anyway? You practically have to take out a loan from the bank to be able to afford all the ingredients to make one and then you need to take time off work to make it—like you could afford to do it now that you bought all the stuff!

How would I know this, hater of fruitcake that I am? My mother made them. My mom was a follower of "I Am Woman, Hear Me Roar" Helen Reddy. Oh sure, she'd gripe about her lot in life and the oppression of being a woman, but come Christmas, she was elbowing the little old ladies out of the way in the grocery store to get herself a stash of artificially colored candied fruits.

It was a long, arduous process making this confounded recipe—one that is still to this day shrouded in maternal mystery. One that required a lot of muttering and deciphering of a recipe obviously passed down before the ballpoint pen was invented. One that required an expensive trip to the liquor store.

But at last the creation was done—fruitcake to be proud of. Fruitcake to be fed to the dog under the table and hidden in napkins and dumped in the trash when no one was looking. And fruitcake to be given as gifts, as relieved luck would have it.

I will say that there are those who do like their hideous fruitcakes—who, like my mother, have muttered over their own ancestral favorite recipe for years. They are rare, albeit they do exist. But if you are like me, an avowed hater of fruitcake, what do you do with the wretched thing after the holidays are over and you have taken down the tree—its semi-final resting place?

Here are some suggestions gleaned from Party411.com so you don't have to eat a bite or feel guilty about leaving your fruitcake in a landfill to decompose for the next 100 years:

- Trivet—self-explanatory
- Centerpiece—put on the table center atop a bed of pine cones, holly, and evergreen branches
- Guest towel holder—place two fruitcakes side by side; insert popsicle sticks to hold your favorite guest towels; decoupage them if you feel up to it
- Knife rest—cut the fruitcake into rectangles and put one at each place at the dinner table; your guests will marvel at your creativity
- Place card holder—cut the fruitcake into rectangles and make a small groove in the top to hold your card; coat with Polyurethane so you can use year after year
- Holiday door knocker—superglue a hinge to the fruitcake bottom and use removable double-stick tape to attach the back of the hinge to your door
- Punch bowl ring—freeze your fruitcake in a block of ice and throw it in your punch bowl for an unusual, yet attractive, garnish.

Some friends offered some other uses:

- A creative doorstop
- A fire starter for the really-doused-with-rum ones
- Contract with the local Mafia to use fruitcakes instead of concrete overshoes
- Need a white elephant gift? (another self-explanatory item)
- Attach fruitcake to the other end of a teeter-totter so your child can use the equipment by him- or herself
- Try Galileo's gravity/acceleration experiment using different brands of fruitcake (science teachers, take note)

I had a few ideas myself:

- Roofing material—having just invested in a partial redo of a roof, I see no difference in materials
- Paperweight—I know it's big, but you haven't seen what is on my desk
- Dumbbells—who needs a gym membership when two fruitcakes work just as well?
- Centerpiece—I know Party411 came up with that already, but why just make a centerpiece for the Christmas holidays? If you Polyurethane it, you could keep changing the decor on it—like hearts for Valentines, flags for the Fourth of July . . . you get the picture
- Building material—thinking of putting an addition on the house? It wouldn't be too difficult to get a collection of them and get your addition for almost free; put an ad in the classifieds saying you'll be happy to (literally) house homeless fruitcakes

Take my word for it—I think that's it. I have spent far too long dwelling on postholiday uses for fruitcakes. Let's hope so anyway.

CINCHY CHRISTMAS DECOR

The arts and crafts world abounds with projects this time of year—as *if* you need one more thing to do. Unplug yourself from the glue gun and take a look at what you can do without all the bewildering crafts.

Hit the dollar store and binge on votive candles and their holders. Personally, I go for unscented votives as opposed to the cheap smell of artificial elderberry or pine boughs—they give me a headache just thinking about them. Remember, you're going for volume and mood.

Go outside and grab yourself some pine cones. If you don't have any in the yard, you can buy them inexpensively at a (gulp) craft store. Go early in the morning, run in, get your cones, and get out of there as quick as you can in case you are inexplicably drawn to a project that will eat up all your waking hours during this festive time. The Christmas holidays can be enjoyable when we aren't consumed with the notion of turning them into a production to rival a Hollywood set.

Get an ordinary can of gold metallic spray paint and spray half the cones. The other half, keep natural. In other words, if you have thirty cones, fifteen will be natural, the other fifteen completely golden. While in the craft store, pick up some flat glass beads in either colors or clear.

In the middle of the table and on your sideboard, arrange some cones and votives and sprinkle the glass beads along the way. At night, when all the candles are lit, it is exquisitely beautiful, and so easy to do. You might need to move parts of your decor to accommodate dinner, but it's relatively simple to move and the effect is simply gorgeous.

The Timeline

TWO WEEKS TO TEN DAYS AHEAD

Call to confirm your guests and family.

Go through your grocery list and buy everything you need for dinner except the fresh stuff. If you're going to do Christmas cookies this year, make the dough now and freeze it for easy baking at a later date. These little do ahead tips are what make the holidays a whole lot less stressful!

Remember to hit the grocery store at an off time, preferably early in the morning when everything is freshly stocked. Make sure you have your list, check it twice, and leave the kids at home. This is not the time to be distracted and arguing with your child over why you won't buy him the mutant sugar ninja cereal that he wants sooooo bad.

Press all linens and napkins, hang them in your closet on a hanger or fold gently, and place back in the sideboard.

And don't forget to double-check the serving pieces you're going to need for your Christmas dinner. You might want to call now and beg, borrow, or steal (just kidding on the last one) the utensils or serving pieces you're going to need. Remember, it's a colossal drag to not have what you need the day of the event! Get it taken care of ahead of time.

ONE WEEK AHEAD

This is the time to go over your list once more. Everything should be bought (except the last-minute fresh stuff), and you should have your ducks or roast, for that matter, in a row. Double-check, double-check, double-check!

Now, go get your fridge cleaned out. I mean really cleaned out, mercilessly cleaned out. A serious scouring of your fridge will help you to have ample room come time to stock with the fresh stuff you will be buying in the next few days. If you need more fridge space, don't discount your cooler sitting in the garage waiting for summer. Clean that thing out, buy some ice, and put it to good use.

THREE DAYS AHEAD

Just like for Thanksgiving, we're going to pull out all of the serving pieces. Write what is going into what and with what on a 3 × 5 card.

For example, note which serving bowl is for mashed potatoes, with serving spoon, and throw it into the bowl with the spoon inside. Once you have everything laid out in front of you, you can stack your serving dishes and the serving utensils separately. Still, leave the 3 × 5 card in the serving piece and place on the dining room table if you're not going to be using it. As you did with Thanksgiving, throw a clean sheet over the top so you can keep everything dust free.

TWO DAYS BEFORE

Purchase the remaining fresh items and pick up your roast if you ordered it from a butcher.

Make the Crème Anglais (page 62) that goes with the Easy Trifle. Once the Crème Anglais has cooled, put a piece of plastic wrap over the top to stop a skin from forming.

THE DAY BEFORE

You can begin prepping your veggies. Place the washed green beans in a zipper-topped bag. If you have enough room in your fridge, you can even prep the butternut squash and put it in the pan, ready to go, covered with plastic wrap so all you have to do is remove the plastic and cook. (You should let it sit to nearly room temperature before popping it into the oven.)

Set your Christmas dinner table and again, using that same sheet, cover your table to keep the dust off.

Sit down, put your feet up, and, once again, go over your plan for dinner. You should have all your T's crossed and I's dotted by now. There is still much to do undoubtedly—this is Christmas Eve, after all. Aren't you glad dinner is completely under control?

Christmas Day Countdown

IN THE MORNING

Get the short ribs roasting, and then make the stock out of the bones, following the directions for the Pan Gravy (page 55).

If you haven't done so already, prepare the Roasted Butternut Squash (page 58).

Prepare the potatoes for Old-Fashioned Mashed Potatoes (page 57). Place in a pot with cold water. Set aside, but again, not on the stovetop or the pot will get warm and begin cooking the potatoes prematurely.

Put the butter, salt, and pepper (if not already there) on the table. Consider two butters and two sets of salt and peppers, one on either end of the table.

Clean as you go! Starting each little cooking spurt with a clean kitchen makes all the difference. Before you start up, run a sink full of hot, soapy water and dump stuff in there as you use it. If necessary, run the dishwasher and empty it after you're nearly finished with all the last-minute preparations.

Remember to rest up a bit. You've got company coming and a full day ahead. No need to burn out before the guests even get there!

TWO AND A HALF HOURS BEFORE

Preheat your oven and place the roast in the oven to cook, following directions for the Roast Beast recipe (page 52). Don't forget to use your most important piece of equipment of the day: meat thermometer.

Make the Creamed Horseradish (page 54).

Make the Easy Trifle (page 61). Loosely place plastic wrap on the top. Remember to keep the custard (Crème Anglais) separate. Pour the custard into a serving pitcher and again, place a small piece of plastic wrap on the top to prevent a skin from forming.

Set up your coffeemaker for after-dinner coffee so all you have to do is flick the switch.

ONE HOUR BEFORE

Your beast should be about halfway through its cooking time. Double-check on the temperature (that means, check the meat thermometer), but for sure, don't keep opening and closing the oven door. When you do, the oven loses heat, causing your cooking time to be way off. Be judicious in your oven openings and closings.

Place the Roasted Butternut Squash into the oven to roast with the beef.

Cook the potatoes for Old-Fashioned Mashed Potatoes and place in a Crock-Pot on low when completed. (See note on testing your Crock-Pot on page 18 before trying this!)

Make the gravy (page 55).

Cook the Sautéed Green Beans with Nutmeg (page 59). Keep warm until serving time.

Heat the rolls.

After your roast has rested, carve the meat and place on the serving platter.

TIME TO EAT!

Put everything in its proper serving dish: beef on the serving platter with the meat fork, rolls in the basket (or baskets) with the napkin to keep them warm, gravy in its boat, green beans, butternut squash, creamed horseradish, and, of course, the mashed potatoes in their bowls or platters.

You've earned the praise you're bound to get. Sit back, enjoy the meal and your guests, and do remember to join hands with those you love and give thanks.

Living with Leftovers

Let's say for the sake of leftovers, you doubled up on your beef. That's a smart thing to do. Leftover roast beast is a primo asset to have in your fridge. Why? Well, the leftovers are totally awesome. Here are a few favorites.

SHEPHERD'S PIE

1 tablespoon olive oil
1 large onion, chopped
1 large carrot, chopped
3–4 cups chopped roast beast
½ teaspoon crushed rosemary
½ teaspoon garlic powder
Salt and pepper to taste
1–2 cups leftover beef gravy
3 cups leftover mashed potatoes

Preheat the oven to 375 degrees.

In a large skillet, heat the olive oil and sauté the onion and carrot till wilted. Add the beef, rosemary, garlic, and salt and pepper. Add the gravy, heat the mixture, and stir together for a minute or two till well mixed.

In a pie plate, spread the beef mixture on the bottom of the pan and then spread the leftover mashed potatoes on top.

Place the pan in the oven and bake for 30 minutes, or until hot and bubbling.

Serve with baby peas and some leftover butternut squash, if you have some.

BEEFY SUBS

Serves as many as you can

Au jus envelope mix
Hoagie rolls or sub rolls, sliced in half, but not separated
Leftover creamed horseradish
Leftover beef, thinly sliced

Make the au jus according to the directions on the back of the envelope. Keep warm.

Heat the rolls if you like and then spread with creamed horseradish. Pile the beef on and serve with a cup of heated au jus. Serve with coleslaw and baby carrots on the side.

NEW YEAR'S EVE

The very idea of throwing a party, let alone *the* party of the year—a New Year's Eve party—can push even the most stalwart into panic mode.

Believe it or not, you can do this easily. Have I ever let you down? All you need are the hints, helps, and—especially—some great recipes that will make you look like Martha (pre–Camp Cupcake), when in fact you were out having your nails done an hour before party time. Now, *that's* a good thing!

So let's get started. First, you need to make a list and check it twice. You knew I'd say that, didn't you? All good parties necessarily start with a guest list, and making sure that it is well thought out and thorough are especially important. You don't want to peeve your boss or a colleague by accidentally excluding him or her from your bash.

Second, your New Year's Eve party is going to be an open house, so you're off the hook as far as protocol for a "real" party, requiring at least two weeks' notice. You can even e-mail your invitations for this informal affair. And because you are ingeniously having an open house, there's no need to worry about those pesky RSVPs. Are you loving this so far?

Open houses are drop-in affairs that don't call for the big whoop-de-do that other parties require. However, you still have some decisions to make regarding the time and length. In my way of thinking, three hours is plenty. And make it between meals, too, so that people won't mistakenly think your open house hors d'oeuvres are their open-mouthed dinner. Between 2:00 and 5:00 in the afternoon ought to do the trick. Though typical New Year's parties are late-night affairs, there are plenty of people who will appreciate the opportunity to drop in, wish you a happy New Year, and then either head home for an early evening (and forgo the dreaded New Year's Eve driving) or do the party animal thing and attend another soiree. Either way, the open house gig is the way to go if you're the host!

Next, you will want to decide on your menu. That's the easy part—I've got it all right here: no fuss, no muss. Most of the ingredients and menu items can be bought at the warehouse store and the rest is so easy, you can even train your dog to do it (assuming he can drive, of course). Instead of thinking of yourself as the cook, see yourself as the Grand Poobah of Shopping. Almost everything you're going to need you will buy and arrange. Cool, huh? Just make sure you set your appointment with your manicurist—that will be harder than doing this menu.

You should probably count on about an 80 percent show from your guest list. They will eat plenty, even without the mealtime timing, so make sure you have enough food. For each item, make sure you can restock the dish three to six times, depending on how many people you have invited, obviously. Keeping the buffet table stocked and sumptuous is the key to a great open house.

CINCHY AND CHINTZY DECOR

Lest you think I'm lazy (let's put that one to rest—I am), this particular party couldn't be easier to decorate for. To be honest, there is nothing to decorate. You don't need those cheesy cocktail napkins that say "Happy New Year" any more than you need streamers, confetti, or noisemakers. Your party is an open house, not a hoedown, and it's being held during the daylight hours.

My advice is to leave your Christmas or Hanukkah stuff in place and use plain white cocktail napkins (unless you have some holiday leftover napkins to use up) and call it a day. Haven't you done enough decorating?

Since I am an Episcopalian, Christmas continues until Epiphany, so I have a ready-made excuse. You can use that one, too, if you like; just save yourself the hassle and headache and use what you have left over from the holidays. I'd skip the jack o'lanterns, however.

The Menu

1. ASSORTED CHEESES, NUTS, CRACKERS, AND FRUIT; OLIVES, MARINATED ARTICHOKE HEARTS, MUSHROOMS, AND SO ON

2. TORTILLA CHIPS WITH SALSA AND GUACAMOLE AND BLACK BEAN DIP

3. SMOKED SALMON CREAM CHEESE

4. VEGETABLE PLATTER AND PITA TRIANGLES WITH DIPS

5. ASSORTED MINIATURE QUICHES

6. ASSORTED MINIATURE SANDWICHES

7. TORTELLINI SKEWERS

8. ASSORTED CHRISTMAS COOKIES

9. ASSORTED QUICK BREADS: ZUCCHINI BREAD, BANANA BREAD, AND PUMPKIN BREAD

10. BROWNIES

11. EGGNOG, PUNCH, ASSORTED DRINKS

THE SHOPPING LIST

All warehouse stores are not created equal, so it's a tough assignment to make up a grocery list for this party. There are two lists here: one for the warehouse and one for the grocery store. Try to get as much as you can at the warehouse store, with the exception of items that, if left over, will just be too ponderously oversized for your house afterwards (unless you relish the idea of a gallon of mayo in your fridge). Try to be flexible with these lists—if the warehouse store doesn't have marinated artichoke hearts, but carries two types of olives, get those instead.

Above all, understand that the spirit of this party is to have easy-to-prepare, easy-to-replenish foods. For the most part, the cooking is at a real minimum. So it's all about ease of accomplishment. Keep that in mind as you

You have no idea how many times I have answered that question. As a caterer, I would be asked about quantity with every party I did, especially open houses and cocktail parties. At these kinds of parties, the main thing are the hors d'oeuvres. Think in terms of how you are feeding everyone. With the number of items on your menu, you want about two to three servings per person. That means you need two to three servings of each item per guest. Your party is not at meal time, so you're off the hook quantity-wise. But understand that there will always be some heavy grazers; you can count on that, so stock up on the stuff you know will be popular.

If you were doing your party at a meal time, I would tell you to have triple the amount I am mentioning here. There is nothing more tragic at a party than running out of food. You want to avoid that at all costs.

head out to the store with these lists (and don't forget to read through the recipes and the warehouse/grocery lists before you go).

AT THE WAREHOUSE

MEAT
Sliced turkey and ham
Smoked salmon

CONDIMENTS
Olives
Marinated artichoke hearts
Marinated mushrooms
Salsa

PRODUCE
Broccoli florets
Cauliflower florets
Baby carrots
Cherry tomatoes
Red bell peppers
Green bell peppers
Yellow bell peppers
Ready-made veggie dips

DAIRY
Assorted cheeses—slices, wedges
2 (8-ounce) packages cream cheese

DRY GOODS
Tortilla chips
Assorted nuts
Assorted dried fruit
Crackers

FROZEN FOODS
1 to 2 (48-ounce) bags assorted miniature quiches
1 to 2 (32-ounce) bags cheese tortellini
Guacamole
Ice

BAKERY
Assorted miniature bread rolls
Assorted quick breads (zucchini, banana, pumpkin, etc.)
Brownies
Cookies

BEVERAGE
Eggnog
Punch
Assorted sodas

OTHER
Disposable serving trays
Paper plates
Plastic cups
Cocktail napkins
Toothpicks—extra-long and regular size
Plastic Wrap

AT THE GROCERY STORE

CONDIMENTS

Mayonnaise

Dijon mustard

Other mustards—your choice

Italian dressing

Commercial oil spray (unless you are using an oil spritzer
    with your own oil)

PRODUCE

Any veggies/fruit of your choice not available at
    warehouse store

CANNED GOODS

1 (4-ounce) can chopped green chiles

1 (15-ounce) can black beans

SPICES

Garlic powder

Ground cumin

Cayenne pepper

DRY GOODS

3 (8-ounce) bags pita bread

BAKERY

Any items not available at warehouse store (cookies,
    quick breads, etc.)

BEVERAGE

Eggnog, or any items not available at warehouse store

TOOLS OF THE TRADE

Serving trays (you will need several—make a count)

Platters

Bowls and spoons for condiments

Small containers for toothpicks

Baskets

Linen napkins (basket liners)

Cheese (butter) knives

Oil spritzer (if not using commercial oil spray)

Ice bucket(s)

Blender

Electric mixer

NEW YEAR'S RESOLUTION OR EVOLUTION?

Making New Year's resolutions wasn't an American idea. Back in the ancient world, Babylonians made their New Year's resolutions, most often to return borrowed farm equipment to their neighbors.

Since the start of a new year signifies a new beginning, goals of losing weight, getting organized, or quitting smoking are frequently the most common resolutions. The number of people who actually keep those resolutions? Well, let's just say that 85 percent of yearly resolution-makers are likely to write the same resolutions year after year. The big-name goal setters and motivational gurus tell us that setting smaller, intermediate goals as steps toward the big goal is the best way to make lasting changes in our lives.

The Recipes

Okay, stay with me for a minute. Let's start with the first item on the list. I've numbered every menu item (page 75) and have a corresponding numbered how-to or recipe for it.

1. This is definitely a warehouse club purchase. Buy all kinds of cheeses—whole bries and sliced cheeses—and arrange on large trays (buy disposables at the same warehouse store). Use the nuts and crackers and fruit (dried and fresh), olives, and marinated mushrooms and artichoke hearts to make your cheese platters elegant. Make three platters for the afternoon and change them every hour, with stuff to restock them (like crackers, fruit, etc.). Don't panic if guests seem to be plowing through the cheese. Just move things around a little to fill in the gaps. (We caterers call that "refreshing" the buffet.)

2. These items are definitely warehouse purchases. You can, however, make a killer homemade guacamole if you want, but I'd forgo the toil and trouble, and make an easier bean dip. Here's my Black Bean Dip that can be made two days in advance.

BLACK BEAN DIP

Makes about 2 cups (make in batches if you need several cups)

1 (15-ounce) can black beans, drained and rinsed
1 (4-ounce) can chopped green chiles
¼ cup salsa—your favorite
½ teaspoon garlic powder
½ teaspoon ground cumin
Cayenne pepper (optional)

Put all the ingredients in a blender and whirl away! That's all there is to it. If it isn't spicy enough, throw in some more cayenne pepper (go easy—¼ teaspoon to start) and crank up the garlic powder and cumin, too.

3. Another easy buffet item. This is a no-brainer. Either buy smoked salmon cream cheese from a bagel place or make it yourself. Combine whipped cream cheese and some chopped smoked salmon (the quantity is up to you—to your taste) and whip with an electric mixer (skip the food processor—you don't want it blended!). This is another easy one to make in advance—up to two days.

4. In the produce department, you can buy virtually any veggie cut up and ready to go. Ditto on the dips—grab what you like and, again, make up the platters as you did for the cheese trays. You'll want three easily, with some backup veggies and dips to fill in as necessary.

   Pita chips are a snap to make, and your guests will love them. Simply cut pita breads into six equal pieces, like a pizza. Spray them lightly with an oil spray (I prefer to use an oil spritzer that I fill myself rather than a commercial oil spray, but the latter will work, too) and bake till crisp and brown in a preheated 400 degree oven. They will take only a few minutes, so check them often. Place the chips in baskets lined with napkins.

5. Another fine warehouse purchase! These little quiches are really quite good. Usually the warehouse has spinach cheese, bacon, and seafood quiches. Get a few bags, follow the heating directions, and serve in a basket lined with a holiday napkin or arranged on a tray.

6. These little sandwiches can be made ahead or can be a do-it-yourself thing. (I vote for do-it-yourself.) Here's how to do it: you need a copious amount of assorted dinner rolls, split and put in baskets lined with linen napkins; assorted mustards and mayo, and assorted meats. I'd go with ham and turkey and call it a day. Too many choices will keep your guests hovering over the table and tasting too much of everything!

7. Those frozen cheese tortellinis are a godsend. Simply cook them according to the package instructions, drain them, then marinate overnight in the fridge with Italian salad dressing. In the morning, skewer the little dar-

lings on extra-long toothpicks (two or three to a pick) and arrange on trays. How's that for easy and elegant?

8, 9, and 10. Unless someone has given you homemade cookies, resist the temptation to do the marathon baking thing and just buy them. The same goes for the quick breads and brownies, although I bet you have a fine stash of goodies that people have given you for the holidays. Now is the time to put them on the buffet table and let your visitors deal with the calories. (Like you need any more help in that department!)

11. The beverages should all be store-bought. Don't even *think* about homemade eggnog.

Whew, we did it! Now that wasn't so bad, was it? A full-on party without the killer kitchen sessions. Everyone will be falling all over themselves congratulating you for throwing a spectacular party, and you'll smirk and say a silent thank you to Sam's Club for the help.

The Timeline

Important! Have you made your appointment with the manicurist?

TWO WEEKS TO TEN DAYS AHEAD

Send out invitations by your choice of delivery—snail mail, e-mail, telephone. Remember: Open houses are informal gatherings and you don't have to adhere to strict rules, including RSVPs.

ONE WEEK AHEAD

Plan the table. If you're using linen tablecloths and napkins, do they need pressing? Press them now and hang them or fold them for later. Double-check your serving pieces and utensils. Arrange to buy or borrow what you need now.

THREE DAYS AHEAD

Clean out your refrigerator to make room for the items from tomorrow's mammoth shopping trip. Check to see if you have a clean, large cooler available for ice storage.

TWO DAYS AHEAD

It's time to shop at your friendly neighborhood warehouse store! Double-check the list against the menu.

Prepare the Black Bean Dip (page 81) and refrigerate.

THE DAY BEFORE

Shop at your favorite grocery store for any items not available at the warehouse store.

Pull out all the pieces you are going to use for serving. Write what is going into or on each piece on a 3 × 5 card and toss the cards into or onto the serving pieces. This will prevent any guesswork on the day of your party. Arrange your table and cover with a clean sheet to keep it dust free.

Get your nails done (or do it the day of).

New Year's Day Countdown

TWO HOURS AHEAD

Send someone out for ice, then arrange appropriate beverages in ice tubs or buckets.

ONE HOUR AHEAD

Arrange the buffet table. Remove the sheet from the table and fill the serving pieces according to your plan.

VALENTINE'S DAY CHOCOLATE FEAST

There is nothing more intoxicating, heady, rich, or sexy than . . . chocolate. (What? You thought I was going to say Brad Pitt?) Remember, men are mere mortals; chocolate is eternal.

Chocolate is in a class by itself. Truly, if there were any justice in the food world, chocolate would have its own food group. My thighs and I have lobbied hard for this one. We weigh in heavily pro-chocolate, to be sure.

When I was pregnant with my first child and had devoured every book on the subject of motherhood, I heard tell that commonly loved foods could turn potentially nauseating when a woman is pregnant. In a strange, love-hate sort of way, I was hoping for instant disdain for chocolate with both pregnancies that would be my ticket out of an obsession. At least, then, I would be free of my hopeless addiction. And I could blame *all* my weight gain on my pregnancy! However, no such luck. At this point in my life, rather than continue to fight a losing battle, I've given in to chocolate—and I suggest you do the same. No use wasting another minute trying to figure out what it takes to give up chocolate. Believe me—been there, done that. All you will get for your trouble is a mean hankering for a Kit-Kat bar.

Chocolate is truly the food of the gods. It is the cure for all things wrong in the world, the stuff that dreams are made of, and the way most women have made it through all thirty-one days of the month, if you know what I mean.

And don't forget that Valentine's Day is precisely the occasion that should be celebrated in an over-the-top, indulgent chocolate feast. We're talking chocolate for breakfast, lunch, and dinner—with Godiva snacks in between. You walk about with a telltale ring around your mouth that lets everyone identify you as a full-blown addict. Completely hopeless, a mainliner with no expectation of recovery.

So let's go with it, shall we? But before we begin, for those whose preference is vanilla over chocolate (yes, there are vanilla people out there), let's give those who aren't in the know a little primer on chocolate. Here are a few rules that will help them cope with the chocoholics in their lives.

1. To err is human, but if you mess with my chocolate, you're history.
2. Chocolate-"flavored" anything is an abomination. Only real chocolate will suffice.
3. If it's imported, in a gold box, and cost a week's salary, we'll follow you anywhere.
4. National Chocolate Day. Used to be once a month but now anything goes. Be prepared.
5. Hershey's Kisses, human kisses—if you're sensitive, don't ask which ones we want.

You can buy all the wonderful imported chocolate you want (or drop not-so-subtle hints so your darling will pick up a skiploader full). The deal is, if you want to really experience chocolate (and isn't that what Valentine's Day is all about anyway?), you must cook with it, bake with it, and then eat it nonstop until February 15. Only then will you come up for air and will probably be suffering from a severe chocolate hangover. Don't come running to me about it—I will be in my own chocolate-induced coma.

Here are the guiltiest, most decadent chocolate recipes in the world. They will truly knock your socks off and the socks of your next-door neighbor, too. If you're a relatively young addict, go easy. Do only one or two of these recipes, eat yourself silly, and close the book. Then take a week off. Come back and then try another few recipes. If you've been "using" for a while, go nuts. I will see you in the ICU— you'll know me by my glassy eyes and the melted Lindt chocolates they couldn't pry out of my hand.

HEART TO HEART

Decorating for Valentine's Day is easy: think red, think hearts, think flowers. Yeah, naturally there is chocolate to take into consideration, but you don't need to be buying any extracurricular chocolates for Valentine's. We've quite done in you and anyone else who will be enjoying this chocolate buffet.

Flowers are always right, and if you have an extra wad of cash, buy red roses to say "I love you" to that special some- one. Or use those red roses to decorate with, and don't discount red rose petals, either. They make a beautiful table decor, mixed with glass beads and all your chocolate desserts in all their chocolicious glory. Just make sure you use your pretti- est serving platters and footed trifle bowls for the Chocolate Bread Pudding. The assorted heights and shapes of all things chocolate will make your buffet sumptuous and beautiful.

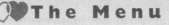

The Menu

DOUBLE-CHOCOLATE HAZELNUT BROWNIES

CHOCOLATE TURTLE PIE

CHOCOLATE PEANUT BUTTER BARS

CHOCOLATE BREAD PUDDING

TRIPLICIOUS CHOCOLATE CHEESECAKE

REAL HOMEMADE CHOCOLATE PUDDING

CHAMPAGNE AND CHOCOLATE MARTINIS

SPARKLING WATERS, ASSORTED SODAS, AND COFFEE
(DECAF, TOO)

THE SHOPPING LIST

CHOCOLATE STUFF

Unsweetened chocolate squares (2 squares)

2 (7-ounce) bags semisweet chocolate chips

Mini chocolate chips (4 tablespoons)

Unsweetened cocoa (6 tablespoons)

Chocolate syrup (¼ cup)

Chocolate graham crackers (16 crushed)

Chocolate cookie wafer crumbs (25 crushed)

1 (4-ounce) bar quality milk or semisweet chocolate
(Lindt is good)

Semisweet chocolate (3 squares)

DAIRY

Butter (1½ cups)

Eggs (9)

Milk (2 cups)

Half-and-half (1⅓ cups)

Whipping cream (3 cups)

Sour cream (½ cup)

3 (8-ounce) packages cream cheese

DRY GOODS

Sugar

Brown sugar

Confectioners' sugar

All-purpose flour

Baking soda

Baking powder

Chopped peanuts, unsalted (½ cup)

Chopped hazelnuts (1 cup)

Chopped pecans (½ cup)

OTHER

Peanut butter, smooth (⅓ cup)

Vanilla extract (6 teaspoons)

30 vanilla caramels

1 loaf French bread

Toothpicks

Plastic wrap

TOOLS OF THE TRADE

Double boiler

Electric mixer

Custard/pudding cups (need 8 or more for 2 recipes)

8-inch square pan

9-inch pie plate

9 × 13-inch baking pan

8-inch springform cake pan

Martini glasses

Champagne glasses

Martini shaker

THE CHOCOLATE BAR

♡💜 Is there anything more decadent, more over-the-top than a chocolate martini? Where high-octane spirits meet high-octane confection? I cannot claim not to have tried a chocolate martini (I have), nor can I say I didn't like it (I did). I just wouldn't recommend it for anyone having to operate machinery (even a blender) after consuming more than one. These babies aren't kind to your liver.

If you still want to make them, make sure you have cabs or a sleepover planned for the evening. Next, follow these instructions for the ultimate chocolate concoction!

4 ounces (½ cup) chocolate liqueur
3 ounces (6 tablespoons) vodka
1 bar cold semisweet chocolate, grated with a potato peeler to make curls

In a cocktail mixer full of ice, combine the chocolate liqueur and vodka. Shake vigorously and strain into two chilled martini glasses. Garnish with chocolate shavings.

DOUBLE-CHOCOLATE
HAZELNUT BROWNIES

Makes 20, just enough for 1 person

2 squares unsweetened chocolate
½ cup butter
2 eggs
1 cup sugar
¾ cup all-purpose flour, sifted
½ teaspoon baking powder
¼ teaspoon salt
1 cup hazelnuts, chopped
1 teaspoon vanilla extract
1 cup semisweet chocolate chips

Preheat the oven to 350 degrees. Lightly grease an 8-inch square pan.

In a double boiler, melt the chocolate with the butter. Cool. Add the eggs and sugar, and beat until well blended (if you don't allow the chocolate butter mixture to cool sufficiently, your eggs will begin to cook).

In a bowl, combine the flour, baking powder, and salt. Stir the flour mixture a bit at a time into the chocolate mixture. Add the hazelnuts and vanilla. Spread the mixture evenly in pan. Sprinkle the chocolate chips on top.

Bake for 25 to 30 minutes. Stick a toothpick in the middle and pull out. If it comes out clean, the brownies are done. Cool 10 minutes (if you have amazing self-control) and cut into squares with sharp knife.

CHOCOLATE TURTLE PIE

Serves 12

CRUST

1½ cups chocolate wafer crumbs (about 25 wafers; smash in a
plastic bag with a rolling pin)
¼ cup butter, melted

FILLING

30 vanilla caramels
2 tablespoons butter
2 tablespoons water
½ cup chopped pecans, toasted
6 ounces cream cheese, softened
⅓ cup confectioners' sugar
1 (4-ounce) bar milk or semisweet chocolate (I like Lindt for this
one)
3 tablespoons hot water
1 teaspoon vanilla extract

TOPPING

2 cups whipping cream (no fake whipped stuff in a tub!)
2 tablespoons confectioners' sugar

Preheat the oven to 350 degrees.

In a large bowl, mix the cookie crumbs and melted butter. Press the mixture firmly against the side and bottom of a 9-inch pie plate. Bake for 10 minutes and set aside to cool.

In a medium pot over medium heat, melt the caramels, butter, and water, stirring frequently until caramels are completely melted. Pour into the crust. Sprinkle with pecans. Refrigerate about 1 hour, until chilled.

Beat the cream cheese and ⅓ cup sugar until smooth. Spread over caramel layer; refrigerate.

Heat the chocolate and hot water in a double boiler over medium-low heat, stirring constantly, until chocolate is melted. Cool to room temperature. Add the vanilla.

With electric beaters, beat the whipping cream and sugar in a chilled medium bowl until stiff, but don't overbeat. Reserve 1½ cups and set aside. Fold the melted chocolate mixture into the remaining whipped cream. Spread this mixture over the cream cheese mixture. Top this gorgeous pie with the reserved whipped cream. Should there be any remaining pie after dessert (as if!), refrigerate.

CHOCOLATE PEANUT BUTTER BARS

Makes 36 bars

½ cup granulated sugar
⅓ cup packed brown sugar
¼ cup butter, softened
⅓ cup smooth peanut butter
1 teaspoon vanilla extract
1 egg
1¼ cups all-purpose flour
½ teaspoon baking soda
½ teaspoon salt
½ cup chopped peanuts (no salt)
1 (7-ounce) package semisweet chocolate chips

Preheat the oven to 375 degrees. Lightly grease and flour a 13 × 9-inch baking pan.

In a large bowl, mix the sugars, butter, peanut butter, and vanilla. Beat in the egg. Stir in the flour, baking soda, and salt. Mix in the peanuts and chocolate chips, and then spread the dough in the prepared pan.

Bake until lightly browned, 12 to 14 minutes, then cool and cut in bars.

CHOCOLATE BREAD PUDDING

Serves 4

1⅓ cups half-and-half
3 tablespoons sugar
4 teaspoons unsweetened cocoa
1 teaspoon vanilla extract
3 eggs, lightly beaten
3½ cups French bread, cubed (½-inch)
4 tablespoons semisweet chocolate chips, plus more for garnish
4 tablespoons whipped cream

Preheat the oven to 325 degrees.

In a medium bowl, combine the half-and-half, sugar, and cocoa. Stir with a wire whisk until well blended. Add the vanilla and eggs, and stir well. Last, add the bread cubes, stirring until moistened, but don't let it soak.

Lightly grease custard cups with butter. Spoon the bread mixture evenly into the cups and top each with a portion of chocolate chips.

Place the cups in a 9 × 13-inch baking pan. Add hot water to the pan to a depth of 1 inch. Bake for 40 minutes or until a knife inserted in the center comes out clean.

Serve with a dollop of whipped cream and a few chocolate chips on top. Dig in—delicious when hot and the whipped cream is nice and cold.

TRIPLICIOUS CHOCOLATE CHEESECAKE

Serves 12

CRUST

¼ cup butter, melted

1⅓ cups chocolate graham cracker crumbs (16 crackers crushed in
a bag with a rolling pin)

FILLING

1 tablespoon vanilla extract

3 squares semisweet chocolate

¼ cup chocolate syrup

2 (8-ounce) packages cream cheese, softened

1 cup sugar

2 tablespoons unsweetened cocoa

1 teaspoon vanilla extract

¼ teaspoon salt

2 eggs

TOPPING

½ cup sour cream

1 tablespoon sugar

2 teaspoons unsweetened cocoa

Preheat the oven to 350 degrees. Lightly grease an 8-inch spring-form pan.

In a medium bowl, mix the butter and cracker crumbs until well blended. Firmly press the mixture into the bottom and up the side (to about 1 inch) of pan. Bake for 10 minutes and let cool on a wire rack. Turn oven down to 300 degrees.

Combine the vanilla and chocolate in the top of a double boiler. Cook the chocolate mixture over simmering water for 2 minutes or until chocolate is melted, stirring frequently. Remove from heat; add the chocolate syrup and stir until smooth.

In a large bowl, beat the cream cheese at medium speed with a mixer until smooth. Add the sugar, cocoa, vanilla, and salt, beating until smooth. Add the vanilla-chocolate mixture, beating at a low speed until well blended.

Add the eggs one at a time, beating well after each addition. Pour the cheese mixture into the crust and bake for 40 minutes or until almost set.

In another bowl, combine the sour cream, sugar, and cocoa, stirring well. Turn the oven off. Pull the cheesecake out and spread the sour cream mixture over the top of the cheesecake. Let the cheesecake stand for 45 minutes in the oven with the door closed. Remove the cheesecake from the oven, and let cool to room temperature. Cover and chill for at least 8 hours before digging in.

REAL HOMEMADE
CHOCOLATE PUDDING

(Almost as fast as the boxed kind)

Serves 4

1 egg yolk
2 cups milk
¼ cup all-purpose flour or cornstarch
½ cup sugar
2 tablespoons cocoa
⅛ teaspoon salt
1 teaspoon vanilla extract
4 tablespoons mini chocolate chips

In a small bowl, using a wire whisk, mix the egg yolk and milk.

In a saucepan, mix the dry ingredients until well blended. Slowly stir in the milk mixture. Go easy—you don't want it lumpy (use your wire whisk). Heat over low heat and continue to stir until mixture thickens.

Pour into pudding cups. Sprinkle the top with the mini chocolate chips. (They will melt—this is a good thing. Swirl before you inhale.)

Chill or serve warm. Bill Cosby, eat your heart out—*this* is pudding.

The Timeline

At this point, you're probably wondering who on earth would you invite to a chocolate bash such as this? The answer is simple: those who adore chocolate as much as you do. If you're a single gal and you abhor Valentine's Day for all the obvious reasons, invite your other single girlfriends and pig out together. If you're one half of a couple, have a couple's party. The point is sharing the love, right? And we all know nothing says love better than imported silky chocolate.

TWO WEEKS AHEAD
Send invitations to your favorite chocoholics.

ONE WEEK AHEAD

Plan your table. If you're using a linen tablecloth and napkins, do they need pressing? Do it now and hang or fold them for later.

Double-check your serving pieces and utensils against your menu. Make arrangements *now* to buy or borrow what you need.

FOUR DAYS AHEAD

Take your shopping list and go for it!

Firm up your guest list.

THREE DAYS AHEAD

Prepare Double-Chocolate Hazelnut Brownies (page 91) and Chocolate Peanut Butter Bars (page 94). Cool, cut, cover, and refrigerate.

TWO DAYS AHEAD

Prepare Chocolate Bread Pudding (page 95) and Triplicious Chocolate Cheesecake (page 96). Cool, cover, and refrigerate. Stick a few toothpicks in the top of the cheesecake so that the plastic wrap doesn't mess up the topping.

THE DAY BEFORE

Prepare Chocolate Turtle Pie (page 92) and Real Homemade Chocolate Pudding (page 98). Cool, cover, and refrigerate. Repeat toothpick procedure above for the pie. Cool the pudding before covering with plastic wrap.

Decide on an appropriate Valentine-themed table centerpiece and buy the needed items.

V-Day Countdown

ONE HOUR BEFORE

Pull Double-Chocolate Hazelnut Brownies and Chocolate Peanut Butter Bars from refrigerator and arrange on serving platters; re-cover and let stand at room temperature. Make whipped cream for bread pudding, cover, and refrigerate.

Set your table with napkins, forks, and spoons.

BUT IT'S HEALTHY, ALREADY!

🤍 Chocolate soothes the savage beast, as any chocolate addict will tell you, and at long last there is medical proof. Catechins, the antioxidants found in green tea that everyone's been talking about as the greatest anticancer component, is found in greater abundance in chocolate! Four times greater, according to Holland's National Institute of Public Health and Environment.

Leave it to the Dutch— the world's finest chocolate producers—to come up with this research.

ONE-HALF HOUR BEFORE

Preheat the oven to low to warm the Chocolate Bread Pudding. Place in oven, covered with foil, to re-heat (but don't let it dry out!).

TEN MINUTES BEFORE

Remove the Chocolate Turtle Pie and Triplicious Chocolate Cheesecake from refrigerator and slice before placing on the table.

Remove Real Homemade Chocolate Pudding from refrigerator and arrange on a tray before placing on the table.

Remove Chocolate Bread Pudding from oven and put on a trivet before placing on the table. Put a bowl of whipped cream and a spoon next to the bread pudding.

CHEESECAKE CRACKS AND OTHER IMPERFECTIONS

🤍 For the record, I'm over it. The cheesecake imperfections, that is, that plague every cheesecake I've ever made. I don't care what you do to make the cracks go away; it won't work, no matter what anyone says. And they say a lot, from doing a water bath, to not opening the oven the first 30 minutes, to not jarring the cheesecake while baking (as if anyone would think that jarring a cheesecake would help the cooking process!), to longer cooking time, shorter cooking time, higher heat, lower heat, and convection heat. But they're all lying to you because they want you to watch their show, buy their books, or swear an oath of allegiance and join their cult. Don't buy it! Cheesecakes are just natural crackheads. And they're never going to change. They crack, big time.

I know you've seen pictures of gorgeous cheesecakes sans cracking, but let me tell you, those photos are done by food stylists, who patch cracks and cover blemishes to make cheesecakes look picture-perfect. But just remember: it's a picture, not the real deal.

EASTER

C hances are, every Easter morning is the same at your house. There are the requisite candy-stuffed Easter baskets happily half-eaten by eager children before breakfast, a mad dash to get out the door for church without the telltale signs of chocolate bunnies on new outfits, and the grand finale of the day—Easter dinner—sometimes for a cast of thousands.

For many people, this holiday meal means generational favorites served every year: the same ham, the same potatoes, the same dessert.

But for those of you who want to try something new, are bored with the same old thing, or have a delicious rebellious streak when it comes to tradition and cooking, these less traditional recipes are for you!

EASY EASTER DECORATING

The colors of spring are what play on this special holiday: pastel pinks, blues, greens, and yellows. And, of course, so are eggs.

If you have children (or if you're a child at heart), you must make colored eggs. You will find egg-dying kits at any grocery store, and they work the best. I have done obscure dye jobs on my eggs using natural ingredients, but the time and results have been less than satisfactory. Let's face it: you're going to do this once a year, so go for easy! You've got plenty to do with this menu!

Use these beautiful dyed eggs for a decoration on your buffet table. One year, I used my favorite white damask tablecloth, pale pink plates, and large, clear glass vases filled with pastel-colored Easter eggs. The effect was truly dazzling and so very simple to pull off.

🐰 **The Menu**   SERVES 6

EASTER HAM WITH SPICY CRANBERRY RELISH

GLAZED BALSAMIC BABY CARROTS

GREEN BEANS AMONDINE

POPPY AND SESAME SEED ROLLS

TRIPLE-WHAMMY SCALLOPED POTATOES

MINTED BLUEBERRY FRUIT SALAD

LEMON MOUSSE PIE WITH RASPBERRIES

THE SHOPPING LIST

MEAT

1 (6- to 8-pound) bone-in ham, wet cured, smoked,
   spiral cut

CONDIMENTS

Olive oil

Vegetable oil

Balsamic vinegar

1 (5-ounce) bottle prepared cream-style horseradish

Honey

PRODUCE

6 handfuls green beans

1 pound baby carrots

3 pounds Yukon Gold potatoes

2 medium onions

Blueberries (3 cups) or buy frozen

1 pint raspberries

2 large peaches

1 large cantaloupe

1 bunch mint

2 to 3 limes (½ cup juice plus zest)

2 to 3 lemons (¼ cup juice plus zest)

CANNED GOODS

1 (15-ounce) can whole-berry cranberry sauce

1 (8.25-ounce) can crushed pineapple

SPICES

Garlic powder

Nutmeg

DAIRY/DAIRY CASE

Butter

1 pint half-and-half

Heavy cream (1 cup)

1 (8-ounce) package cream cheese

Cheddar cheese (4 cups, shredded)

8 slices Provolone cheese

Romano cheese (1 cup, grated)

1 package Pillsbury roll-out piecrusts (red box or tube)

DRY GOODS

1 (2-ounce) package sliced almonds

1 (¼-ounce) envelope unflavored gelatin

Brown sugar

Confectioners' sugar (1 cup)

All-purpose flour

Superfine sugar

FROZEN FOODS

Blueberries (3 cups), if not buying fresh

Sliced peaches, if not buying fresh

Poppy and sesame seed (or other) dinner rolls, if not
buying fresh

BAKERY

Poppy and sesame seed rolls, or buy frozen

OTHER

Gallon-size zipper-topped plastic bags

Plastic wrap

TOOLS OF THE TRADE

You most likely have everything here. Just in case, here
are a few things you may not have that you might want
to pick up.

Medium to large shallow baking pan

9 × 13-inch baking dish

Wire rack

Electric mixer (either a hand or stand alone mixer)

Basting brush

Wire rack

Carving knife set

Glass serving bowl

The Recipes

EASTER HAM WITH SPICY CRANBERRY RELISH

Serves 12

*1 (6–8 pound) bone-in (shank), fully cooked extra-lean ham,
    precut in a spiral*
1 (15-ounce) can whole-berry cranberry sauce
1 (8¼-ounce) can crushed pineapple, drained
1 (5-ounce) bottle prepared cream-style horseradish

Preheat the oven to 325 degrees.

Place the ham in a shallow baking pan. Bake uncovered for 1 to 1½ hours. Remove ham from the oven, let sit about 10 minutes, and then remove slices for serving. If you're feeling a little less than confident on how to embark upon this carving task, check out the diagram on page 116 that will show you how to position your carving utensils so you can do this easily.

Meanwhile, combine the remaining ingredients in a medium bowl. The horseradish is really strong and will clean out your sinuses in a New York second. You might want to start with half, or even less, of the bottle and add it to taste. Transfer this mixture to a serving bowl and chill until serving time. Serve the relish with the ham.

HAMMING IT UP

In the Dr. Seuss classic *Green Eggs and Ham,* the Cat in the Hat went to great lengths to convince Sam that there was nothing better than green eggs and ham. But how did the Cat know what kind of ham to pick?

That's a question that has plagued many an Easter cook. That and which is the "right" one, as well as what to do with it and will it be too fatty? Here are some tips to help you choose your ham with confidence:

- Shank you, very much. Bone-in hams are much tastier than boneless hams and shank-end bone-in half hams are the best—less fat and gristle. The package will tell you that it is a shank end, but in case it doesn't, look for the one with a pointy end, not a rounded end. Boneless hams may seem easier, but "boneless" means that the ham has had to be reshaped to make it look whole again and the texture isn't nearly as good. Not only that, but the leftover ham bone is the quintessential ingredient for my Splendid Split Pea Soup!

- Read the label. There is a lot to this ham-buying thing. The label should give you a lot of information. They add all kinds of stuff to hams these days; watch for the percentages of water added, juices added, and so on. You want the lowest percentage possible and/or none at all. Just pay attention to what you are buying to make sure you're not paying for 20 percent water or any other liquid.

- I Ham what I Ham. Do you want a wet- or a dry-cured ham? A country ham or a smoked ham? The answer is easy: stick with a wet-cured smoked ham, pre-cut (spiral cut, if you're smart). Country hams are usually dry-cured and are *very* salty and have to be soaked and messed with. Why do that? One year, I accidentally bought a country ham that I heard was so good and skipped the soaking part. It was awful and I bloated terribly the next day! Make it easy, skip the bloating, and get the right ham.

GLAZED BALSAMIC BABY CARROTS

Serves 6

1 tablespoon olive oil
3 cups baby carrots
1½ tablespoons balsamic vinegar
1 tablespoon brown sugar

In a skillet over medium-high heat, heat the olive oil. Sauté the carrots in the oil for about 10 minutes, stirring as you go; they will burn if you leave them alone too long. Stir in the vinegar and brown sugar; mix to coat, cover, and let sit for a few minutes (for flavors to meld), then serve.

GREEN BEANS AMONDINE

Serves 6

6 handfuls green beans (about 1¼ pounds)
1 tablespoon butter (I use unsalted)
Splash of olive oil
Salt and pepper to taste
1 (2-ounce) package sliced almonds
Generous dash of nutmeg (or you can grate it fresh—I have a
   grater and it's awesome!)

When you go to the grocery store, count out by the handful how many beans you will need. Give each adult one handful, and count one handful per two small children. Yes, use your hands, grab a handful of beans, plop it into a plastic bag, and consider it a serving.

Wash the beans and string them (pull the string starting at the stem end and pull to the tip). Then snap them in half (or cut them or leave them whole if they're thin and small). Steam them in a veggie steamer or boil them in a skillet half full of water. When they turn bright green, they're finished (they will still be a little undercooked). Drain them and set aside.

In a skillet, heat the butter and oil over medium-high heat and add the beans. Add the salt and pepper to taste and sliced almonds. Sauté for about 2 to 3 minutes. Add the nutmeg and sauté another minute or so. Beans should be tender, but not mushy.

POPPY AND SESAME SEED ROLLS

Buy them! Make sure they're of a good quality. And *butter*, not margarine.

TRIPLE-WHAMMY
SCALLOPED POTATOES

Serves 12

¼ *cup butter, melted*
1 teaspoon garlic powder
4 cups shredded Cheddar cheese
8 slices Provolone cheese, cut into small pieces
1 cup grated Romano cheese
2 tablespoons flour
3 pounds Yukon Gold potatoes, peeled and thinly sliced
Salt and pepper to taste
2 onions, thinly sliced
1 pint half-and-half

Preheat the oven to 350 degrees. Lightly grease a 9 × 13-inch baking dish. Put the butter in a small bowl, then mix in the garlic powder. In a medium bowl, toss together the cheeses with the flour till the cheese is very lightly coated. You're now ready to assemble your casserole.

On the bottom of the baking dish, layer one third of the potato slices. Drizzle the garlic butter over the top, then add salt and pepper. Now layer one third of the onion slices, followed by the cheese, and then start layering all over again, repeating the process till your ingredients are all gone.

Once you've ended on a cheesy note, drizzle the half-and-half over the top slowly so it seeps into all the layers. Pop the whole thing into the oven and bake till taters are tender and the whole mess is bubbling and fragrant, about 45 minutes or so, depending on how thick you cut your potatoes.

UNRAVELING THE MYSTERY OF MELONS

There are two kinds of people in life: those who pick good melons and those who do not.

We've all seen the good melon pickers at the market or produce stand, circling the pile like an exotic bird beginning an elaborate mating dance. Then, when the moment is right, the melon picker swoops in and begins to thump, smell, and feel the melons. But why all the fanfare and melon exhibitionism?

Because that is how you end up with a perfect melon. And to help you decode what exactly goes on in securing a good melon, here are some tips to unwrap forever the mystery of melons:

- Go for the heavyweights. The heavier the melon, the juicier it is. Pick up two same-size melons and choose the heavier of the two.

- Check the spot. If the melon you are thinking of purchasing is a Persian, cantaloupe, or casaba, it will have a little indentation on the end where it was attached to the vine. The other end is the blossom end, and it is the blossom end, not the indentation, that you should check for a little softness. That's a very common mistake with amateur melon pickers.

- Nice complexion. Certain melons, like honeydew and other smooth-skinned melons, have a light, creamy yellow skin, not greenish blue. They should also have a velvety touch to them. Cantaloupes should look yellow underneath their netted skins, not green.

- Sniff test. A good melon will smell like a good melon. If you pick up a cantaloupe and can't smell it, chances are it was picked too early and though it will soften up, the flavor will never be there.

- Knock, knock. Who's there? Watermelon. Watermelon who? A hollowish-sounding watermelon is a good pick. Ditto on the yellowish underbelly of the dirigible-looking watermelon. Skip the watermelons with white undersides; they've been picked too soon. If the watermelon is cut, it should be firm, not mushy. The flesh should be beautifully colored and the smell potent.

- In season. Summer is prime time to buy melons, although they can be had in the springtime, too. All of these tests will be much easier to administer to an unsuspecting melon if you're doing this mid-summer as opposed to Christmastime.

MINTED BLUEBERRY FRUIT SALAD

Serves 4

MINT DRESSING

½ cup fresh mint leaves, roughly chopped
½ cup vegetable oil
½ cup lime juice
2 tablespoons honey
1 teaspoon zested lime peel
Pinch of salt

SALAD

3 cups fresh or frozen blueberries
2 large peaches, pitted and sliced (or use frozen sliced peaches)
1 large cantaloupe, cut into 1-inch pieces

In a medium bowl, make the dressing by combining all the ingredients and blending well.

Stir in the blueberries, peaches, and cantaloupe pieces. Allow the fruit to marinate for about 30 minutes. Place fruit in a pretty glass bowl and serve.

LEMON MOUSSE PIE WITH RASPBERRIES

Serves 8

1 (¼-ounce) envelope unflavored gelatin
½ cup lemon juice
¼ cup water
1 teaspoon lemon zest
1 (8-ounce) package cream cheese
1 cup confectioners' sugar
1 cup heavy cream
1 9-inch pie shell, pre-baked (see page 114 for timing)
1 pint fresh raspberries
Fresh mint leaves, for garnish

In a saucepan, over medium heat, combine the gelatin, lemon juice, and water, stirring until dissolved. Remove from the heat and add the lemon zest. Set aside and let cool slightly.

In a large bowl, combine the cream cheese and sugar, beating with an electric mixer until smooth. Blend in the cooled gelatin mixture, then refrigerate till thickened, about 15 minutes.

In the meantime, whip the cream till soft peaks form. Bring the cream cheese mixture out of the fridge and carefully fold in the whipped cream. Remember to be gentle; you want to preserve the air that is in the whipped cream. Spoon the filling into your piecrust. Refrigerate an hour or so, or until firm.

HOW TO ZEST A LEMON

Zest gives your dish that certain, um . . . zest. (Sorry, couldn't help myself.) The rind contains a sharp burst of flavor that will add extra punch to whatever you're preparing. It's easy to zest, even if you don't have that handy-dandy apparatus known as a zester. In a pinch, a grater will do. Simply grate the citrus of your choice carefully, making sure you get only the colorful peel and not any of the bitter pith beneath the rind. If your zest is fine enough after grating, there's no need to do anything else. If it is still kind of big, simply take a knife and chop the grated zest to make it finer. The object is to flavor something with a little "extra," not wallop your guests with a citrus clobbering.

PIE CRUST

Okay, I'm a cheater, big time. Yes, I know how to make pie crust, and dang if my pie crust isn't to die for, too. But I also have a life and cannot dedicate myself to the endless pursuit of making yet again another pie crust. So here's what you do: buy it.

You can buy Pillsbury pie crusts ready to go that are just as good as what you can make. Well, almost. Better than frozen ones anyway, and these refrigerated pie crusts are truly the ultimate cheat because you can put them in your own pie plate (no tattletale signs of ready-made here), and pinch and squeeze the crust along the sides just like you do with a homemade crust. You gotta love that.

And to make it even tastier and crisper (which I like), brush the crust with a little water and sprinkle with superfine sugar. This will crisp it up and make it a little sweeter, which is good for this particular recipe.

To serve, place one raspberry on each pie slice, with a mint leaf and about 4 fresh raspberries on the plate.

The Timeline

ONE WEEK AHEAD

If you have a favorite butcher, order your ham now.

Check your linen tablecloth and napkins. If they need pressing, do it now and hang them or fold them for later.

Double-check your kitchen tools, serving pieces, and utensils. If you need to buy or borrow anything, this is the time to do so.

TWO TO THREE DAYS AHEAD

Clean out your refrigerator.

Review your shopping list and buy every item you need. If you've ordered your ham from a butcher, pick that up, too.

THE DAY BEFORE

Wash and string the green beans; steam them as directed in recipe; cool and place them in a large zipper-topped plastic bag; refrigerate.

If using fresh peaches for the Minted Blueberry Fruit Salad, rinse and cut up the peaches and store in a zipper-topped plastic bag; refrigerate. Likewise, if using fresh blueberries, rinse, drain, and store in a separate zipper-topped plastic bag; refrigerate.

Prepare Spicy Cranberry Relish (page 106); cover and refrigerate.

Follow package directions and bake pie crust. Cool on a wire rack, then cover and refrigerate.

Assemble your serving pieces and utensils and designate the item to be served in or on each piece by writing the menu item on a 3 × 5 card and placing it in or on each piece. Stack these platters, bowls, and utensils in one area and cover with a towel to keep dust free.

Set your table and cover with a sheet to keep the dust off.

FOUR HOURS AHEAD

Remove the sheet from your table and check for completeness. Place salt and pepper (if not already there) and butter on the table. Consider two butters and two sets of salt and pepper, one on either end.

TWO HOURS AHEAD

If using frozen blueberries and peaches for Minted Blueberry Fruit Salad, remove them from the freezer, rinse, drain, and set out in separate bowls to thaw.

Assemble Triple-Whammy Scalloped Potatoes (page 110). Preheat the oven to 325 degrees. Peel the potatoes and slide each potato into a bowl of cold water to prevent it from turning brown while peeling the remainder. Pat each potato dry before slicing. Proceed with recipe directions.

Place ham and potatoes in preheated oven to bake for approximately 1 to 1½ hours.

ONE HOUR AHEAD

Remove the green beans from the refrigerator and bring to room temperature.

Prepare filling for Lemon Mousse Pie (page 113) and refrigerate, uncovered, to set.

Check bathrooms to make sure you have clean guest towels and extra toilet tissue available.

ONE-HALF HOUR AHEAD

Remove towel from serving pieces.

Assemble Minted Blueberry Fruit Salad (page 112); place in designated serving bowl and refrigerate until ready to serve.

Check on ham and potatoes in oven. If they are cooked, remove the ham from the oven. Keep the potatoes in the oven and crank the temperature up to 425 degrees and continue to cook until lightly brown on top, 5 to 10 minutes; then remove from oven.

FIFTEEN MINUTES AHEAD

Start preparing Green Beans Amondine (page 109) and Glazed Balsamic Baby Carrots (page 108).

TIME TO EAT!

Place the finished dishes in/on their designated serving pieces.

Remove the fruit salad and relish from refrigerator.

Dinner is served!

Loving the Leftovers

Ham is a well-loved leftover and for the most frugal cook, it gets used to the bitter end, including the ham bone, which makes split pea soup that will positively bring tears to a soup lover's eyes. Here are some wonderful recipes to help you use up your ham surplus.

CREAMY PASTA WITH HAM

Serves 6

1 pound corkscrew pasta
2 tablespoons butter
1 small onion, finely chopped
4 garlic cloves, pressed
1 pound mushrooms, sliced
1 teaspoon oregano
2 teaspoons basil
½ to 1 teaspoon crushed red pepper (depending on your heat index)
1½ cups chopped leftover ham (remove any fat before chopping)
1½ cups half-and-half
1 cup spaghetti sauce (your favorite)
1 cup frozen baby peas, thawed
Grated Romano cheese, for garnish

Cook the pasta according to package directions. When done, drain and cover with dishtowel to keep warm.

In the meantime, in a large skillet, melt the butter over medium heat. Add the onion and garlic and cook until softened. Stir in the mushrooms, oregano, basil, and red pepper. Cook until the liquid from the mushrooms has evaporated. Add the ham and cook for another 4 to 5 minutes.

Pour in the half-and-half and bring to a very light simmer. Stir in the spaghetti sauce and peas. Cook, stirring occasionally, until the sauce has reduced and is nice and thick. Return the drained pasta to the pot that you cooked it in, and scrape all the sauce you just made over the pasta and mix well. Serve with a sprinkling of Romano cheese over the top.

SPLENDID SPLIT PEA SOUP

1 pound split peas
1 leftover ham bone
2 carrots, peeled and diced
1 large onion, chopped
1 celery stalk, chopped
2 quarts water
Salt and pepper to taste
½ teaspoon thyme
½ bay leaf

Combine all the ingredients in a Crock-Pot. Cover and cook on low heat for 8 to 10 hours. If there is any ham left on the bone, remove the ham bone, cut the meat off, dice (and remove any fat), and return meat to soup. Otherwise, just toss the bone.

PASSOVER

Having never attended a Seder supper, I felt somewhat like a (gefilte) fish out of water on this holiday. So I did what any self-respecting goy would do in a situation like this and asked an expert for some help. My dear friend Judy Gruen, a wonderful writer and devout Orthodox Jew, happily obliged and has given a nice thumbnail sketch of what a Seder is all about—the whole nine yards.

Judy is a humor writer and has written a column for *Healthy-Foods*, my weekly e-zine, for a number of years now. She has her own Web site, newsletter, and some hilarious books you will want to check out yourself at www.judygruen.com. Take it away, Judy—

There's an old joke that goes around about the meaning behind most Jewish holidays: They tried to kill us, we won, let's eat! Of course, the truth is far more profound than that. Still, there's no getting around the fact that Passover, perhaps more than almost any other Jewish holiday, becomes food-centered. This is not because we are supposed to eat more (though, heaven help us, we usually do), but because of the requirement on Passover to avoid any *chametz*, or leavened products, or even to let our food or cooking utensils have contact with any chametz.

This explains why Jews who follow the Jewish dietary laws keep separate cookware, dishes, and cutlery that we use only for Passover cooking. (It also explains why we like big kitchens: we have a lot of stuff to store!) Similarly, many food items that are completely kosherific throughout the year may not be kosher for Passover, since they may have ingredients that are not kosher for Passover, such as cornstarch. Some foods won't be kosher for Passover because they were processed on the same cooking equipment as was used to make other foods that are normally kosher, but not for Passover (say, for example, pasta).

THE SEDER PLATE

Passover is, above all, about the miraculous deliverance of the Jewish people after hundreds of years of slavery in Egypt. It is also about learning to understand the concept of true spiritual freedom. A centerpiece of the Seder, both literally and figuratively, is the Seder plate, containing foods that symbolize many facets of the holiday. Here's what you'll need on your Seder plate:

1. A roasted shank bone or turkey bone (*zeroa*), representing the lamb that was offered by the Jews to God on the eve of the Exodus.
2. A bitter vegetable (*maror*), such as grated horseradish or some bitter greens, reflective of our bitter slavery.
3. A root vegetable (*karpas*), such as a boiled potato, yet another symbol of back-breaking labor and the minimal food we had to eat during slavery.
4. An apple-nut-wine mixture (*charoset*), symbolizing the mortar we had to make to build bricks. Although it symbolizes part of our slavery, the *charoset* is a sweet dish that people like to eat along with their matzoh, so make a lot!
5. A roasted egg (*beitzah*), representing the traditional holiday sacrifice that the Jewish high priests used to offer in the ancient Temple of Jerusalem.
6. Romaine lettuce or other bitter vegetable (*chazeret*), also reflective of bitter enslavement.

Of course, Jews don't "break bread" at the Passover Seder—they break matzoh! And because it is (let's be honest here) flat and dry, it breaks very easily! A Seder table will also feature a plate with three unbroken matzohs covered by a special cloth. As the Seder progresses, these matzohs will be eaten, all in due time.

Four cups of wine or grape juice are also drunk during the Seder, so stock up because it will go fast if you have a lot of guests!

—Judy Gruen

If all this sounds confusing, that's because it is—but only at first. Once you get used to dealing with the ins and outs of kosher cooking, it becomes second nature. And when you sit down to a beautiful Seder experience with family and friends, reliving the experience of the Exodus from Egypt, all your efforts will have been well worth it, especially if you follow Leanne's flawless cooking instructions!

The Menu

CHICKEN LIVERS WITH CURRANTS

MATZOH BALL SOUP

CHOPPED APPLE CHAROSET

ROASTED HONEY CARROTS

NANCY'S HUSBAND'S TRADITIONAL BRISKET
   WITH TZIMMIS

SAUTÉED BABY SPINACH

CHOCOLATE FLOURLESS TORTE

THE SHOPPING LIST

The shopping list contains the food for the Seder supper, but not the stuff you'll need to make a Seder plate (see page 120), should you want to make the Seder plate as well, so be sure to add those items to your shopping list.

MEAT
1 pound chicken livers
1 (4-pound) brisket, first cut

CONDIMENTS
Extra-virgin olive oil
Vegetable oil
Corn or canola oil
Kosher red wine (¼ cup)
Honey (2 tablespoons)
Prepared horseradish

PRODUCE
3 pounds onions
1 head garlic
1 bunch parsley

4 large Red Delicious apples

2 (10-ounce) bags washed baby spinach

2½ pounds plus 3–5 large carrots

2 to 4 sweet potatoes (depending on size)

1 pint raspberries

CANNED GOODS

12 cups chicken broth (if not making homemade)

SPICES

Cinnamon

Black peppercorns

Nutmeg

Vanilla extract

DAIRY/DAIRY CASE

Eggs (16 or more)

Margarine (pareve)

DRY GOODS

Currants (½ cup)

Chopped walnuts (2 cups)

Almonds (⅓ cup)

Granulated sugar

Dark brown sugar

Cocoa powder

3 (10-ounce) packages matzoh

BEVERAGE

Wine and/or grape juice

OTHER

Foil wrap

Toothpicks

Plastic wrap

TOOLS OF THE TRADE

Nothing here is very unusual—you may have most or all of these items. This is just a convenient checklist in case you need to buy or borrow something.

Blender/food processor

Large ovenproof pan with cover (Dutch oven)

15½ × ½ × 1-inch jelly-roll pan

Baking sheet

Pepper mill

CHICKEN LIVERS WITH CURRANTS

Makes 3 cups

1 cup coarsely chopped onion
3 tablespoons olive oil
1 pound chicken livers, washed and patted dry
4 eggs, hard-cooked and peeled
½ cup currants
Salt and pepper to taste
1 (10-ounce) package matzoh, to serve

In a skillet, over medium-high heat, saute the onion in half the oil, cooking till nicely browned, about 5 minutes. Remove the onion from the skillet and set aside. Add remaining oil to the skillet, then the chicken livers. Cook until livers are cooked through and well done, but not too rubbery. Add additional oil, if necessary. Cool slightly before the next step.

Using a blender or food processor, finely chop the livers together with the hard-cooked eggs and onion. Now add the currants and mix thoroughly. Place the chicken liver mixture in a serving bowl; add salt and pepper and a splash of olive oil, if needed. Refrigerate till ready to serve.

To serve, place the bowl in the middle of a platter with matzoh around the periphery.

MATZOH BALL SOUP

Serves 8

2 (10-ounce) packages matzoh, broken into small pieces
½ cup margarine (pareve)
6 eggs
Salt and pepper to taste
3 tablespoons minced parsley
2 onions, finely chopped
8 cups chicken broth (homemade is preferable)

In a large pot, over high heat, bring about 8 cups of lightly salted water to a boil.

Break the matzoh into small pieces and place in a large bowl. Add water to cover and allow to soak for a few minutes, until soft. Drain off excess water.

Melt the margarine in a large skillet, over medium heat, and stir in matzoh; stir until the mixture is dry and slightly browned. Set aside and let cool a minute.

Mix in the eggs, salt and pepper, parsley, and onions. Mix just enough to make the mixture hold together. Roll the matzoh into Ping Pong–size balls. Place a ball in the boiling water to test the mixture. The ball must rise to the top of the water and not break apart. If it does not rise, then too much matzoh meal was added. In this case, add another beaten egg to the mixture and try again. When desired consistency is reached, roll all of mixture into similar-size balls.

In a large saucepan, bring the chicken broth to a slow boil over medium heat. Add the matzoh balls and cook. Serve soup as the balls rise to the top of the broth.

CHOPPED APPLE CHAROSET

Serves 8

4 large Red Delicious apples, chopped
2 cups walnuts, finely chopped
2 teaspoons sugar
2 teaspoons ground cinnamon
¼ cup kosher red wine

In a large bowl, mix the apples, nuts, sugar, and cinnamon. Add the wine and thoroughly blend. Refrigerate till serving time.

ROASTED HONEY CARROTS

Serves 8

2½ pounds carrots, peeled and cut on an angle (French cut)
2 tablespoons extra-virgin olive oil
2 tablespoons honey
Salt and pepper to taste

Preheat the oven to 450 degrees.

In a medium saucepan, bring about 3 cups of water to a boil. Add the carrots, reduce the heat to medium, cover, and cook until tender, 5 minutes.

In a large bowl, combine the oil and honey. Drain the carrots, add them to the bowl, and toss with the oil and honey, salt and pepper.

On a baking sheet, place the honey-oil carrots in a single layer (no overlapping) and roast for 25 minutes, then serve.

NANCY'S HUSBAND'S TRADITIONAL BRISKET WITH TZIMMIS

Serves 8

Nancy Miller is the Editor-in-Chief at Ballantine. When it was time to forage for Passover recipes, my editor Caroline came to the rescue with Nancy's husband's brisket recipe that is rumored to be the best brisket in Manhattan. I suppose there is such a thing as a brisket bake-off or another way to determine blue ribbon status, but after reading through this recipe and then testing it myself, I have to tell you that I will go no further than this recipe—every brisket maker from Manhattan to Mississippi and then west, take note: this is blue ribbon brisket.

The time required is about 3 hours in the first version, but 3 hours plus an overnight for the second version.

> *2–3 tablespoons vegetable oil*
> *1 (4-pound) first-cut brisket*
> *Approximately ½ teaspoon salt*
> *10 twists of pepper mill (black pepper)*
> *1 quart chicken stock*
> *½ teaspoon grated nutmeg*
> *3–5 large carrots, cut into large chunks*
> *2–4 sweet potatoes, depending on size, cubed (1½-inch pieces)*
> *⅓ cup dark brown sugar*
> *Prepared horseradish, to serve (optional)*

Choose a large ovenproof pan with cover, such as a Dutch oven. The brisket should fit inside without too much crowding. It will shrink, but you'll need to flip it over, so you can use the space. Heat the pan until hot, then add the oil.

Rinse and pat dry the brisket, then slip it into the hot oil. Brown well, about 10 minutes on each side. Add salt and pepper.

Add the stock, letting it nearly cover the brisket. Allow it to boil rapidly for a minute or so, then turn the heat to a simmer, and cover. Slowly cook for 45 minutes.

In the meantime, turn the oven to 400 degrees.

Remove top of Dutch oven and sprinkle in the nutmeg. Turn the meat over and stir. If a lot of the stock has boiled away, add water to cover.

Add the carrots, sweet potatoes, and brown sugar. Cover and place in oven for 1 hour.

Remove from the oven; spoon the carrots and potatoes into a separate bowl. Place the brisket on a cutting board, and let it sit for about 15 minutes before slicing. Slice across the grain with a long, very sharp knife, making each slice about ⅛-inch thick. Or, for easier slicing and a more attractive presentation, refrigerate the brisket overnight, then slice cold. Reheat with the carrots and potatoes. Serve with horseradish, if you like.

SAUTÉED BABY SPINACH

Serves 8

2 (10-ounce) bags pre-washed baby spinach
1 tablespoon olive oil
2 garlic cloves, pressed
Salt and pepper to taste

In a large skillet or wok, heat half the olive oil over medium-high heat and add 1 garlic clove when the skillet is hot. Add 1 bag of the spinach and stir quickly to heat. Salt and pepper and keep moving the spinach around. As spinach begins to wilt and turn bright green, remove from the skillet, place in a serving bowl, and repeat the process with the remaining oil, remaining garlic, and second bag of spinach.

CHOCOLATE FLOURLESS TORTE

Please read the recipe through before you start making this cake to see how it all works. It's an easy recipe as long as you know what you're doing and what to do when!

> *Vegetable oil*
> *⅓ cup cocoa powder*
> *¼ cup boiling water*
> *3 tablespoons margarine (pareve), softened*
> *1 teaspoon vanilla extract*
> *3 egg yolks*
> *⅔ cup sugar*
> *⅓ cup almonds, finely ground*
> *6 egg whites*
> *1 tablespoon cocoa powder, for dusting*
> *1 pint fresh raspberries, for serving*

Preheat the oven to 350 degrees. Line the bottom of a 15½ × ½ × 1-inch jelly-roll pan with foil extending slightly over sides, and lightly grease the foil with a little oil.

In a small bowl, mix the cocoa and boiling water. Keep stirring until the mixture is smooth. Stir in the margarine and vanilla. Set aside to cool.

Meanwhile, in a large bowl, combine the egg yolks and ½ cup of the sugar. Using electric beaters, beat on medium speed until light and fluffy, about 5 minutes. Add the cooled chocolate mixture and the almonds, beating until well blended.

In another large bowl, beat the egg whites until foamy. Gradually add the remaining sugar and continue to beat until stiff peaks form. Fold one-fourth of the egg whites into the chocolate mixture, then add the remaining whites, folding in carefully. Pour the batter into the prepared pan and bake 18 to 20 minutes, or until the cake springs back when touched lightly in the middle.

When the cake is done, remove from the oven and let cool on a wire rack while still in the pan. Dust with cocoa, then cut into serving pieces and serve, garnished with fresh raspberries.

The Timeline

ONE WEEK AHEAD

If you have a favorite butcher, order your brisket now.

Plan your table. If you are using a linen tablecloth and napkins, do they need pressing? Press them now and hang or fold them for later.

Double-check your serving pieces and kitchen utensils against your menu. Make arrangements now to buy or borrow anything you'll need.

TWO TO THREE DAYS AHEAD

Clean out your refrigerator.

Review your shopping list and buy every item you need. If you've ordered your brisket from a butcher, pick that up, too.

THE DAY BEFORE

If you've chosen the reheat option for the brisket, prepare and cook that now. Allow the cooked brisket to come to room temperature; refrigerate, covered.

Prepare Chicken Livers with Currants (page 125); cover and refrigerate.

Prepare Chocolate Flourless Torte (page 132); then insert a few toothpicks in the top; cover and refrigerate.

Rinse raspberries in cold water; cover and refrigerate. (Don't add berries to torte until serving time.)

Meanwhile, pull all the pieces you are going to use for serving. Write the name of each menu item on a 3 × 5 card and place it in or on that particular serving piece. Then stack your bowls, platters, and other serving pieces together in one area, with the cards in or on them. Cover with a towel to keep them dust free.

Set your table and cover with a sheet to keep any dust off.

FOUR HOURS AHEAD

If you've opted to cook your brisket today, preheat your oven and prepare Nancy's Husband's Traditional Brisket (page 129).

Prepare Chopped Apple Charoset (page 127); cover and refrigerate.

Remove the sheet from your table and check for completeness. Place salt and pepper (if not already there) and margarine on the table. Consider two margarines and two sets of salt and pepper, one on either end.

Remember to clean as you go—keep a sink full of soapy water available and dump stuff in there as used. Run the dishwasher and empty it.

Take a time-out and put your feet up for a while.

Double-check the bathrooms for clean guest towels, hand soap, and extra toilet tissue.

Set up the coffeemaker so all you have to do is flip the switch.

FIFTEEN MINUTES AHEAD

Prepare the Seder plate and place on table.

Remove the Chicken Livers with Currants from refrigerator. Arrange on a platter or tray with matzoh around the periphery.

TIME TO EAT!

Remove the towel from the stack of serving pieces. Place finished dishes in or on their designated pieces.

Ring the dinner bell!

MOTHER'S DAY

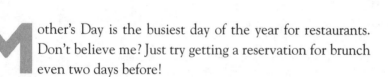

Mother's Day is the busiest day of the year for restaurants. Don't believe me? Just try getting a reservation for brunch even two days before!

It would be commonsensical, I would imagine, to include a brunch menu for Mother's Day, or a breakfast-in-bed menu, but that is too pedestrian for my taste. I think most moms quiver in between their quilts waiting for disaster to happen in the kitchen and would much prefer to get up, go to the bathroom, and have a decent cup of coffee before beginning "their" holiday. The whole "breakfast in bed" idea is cute, but difficult to pull off for the novice. And let's face it: for the most part, dad and his musketeers are pretty much amateurs when it comes to cooking. Asking a father and his progeny to time a perfectly poached egg without destroying the stovetop and to serve, at the same time, crisp toast that is golden brown, lightly buttered, and not burned, is much like teaching quantum physics to preschoolers—pretty incongruent.

To that end, I've remedied this whole conundrum by bagging breakfast and doing an easy dinner. Timing is easier and the menu I've provided is a snap to pull off. Someone else doing dinner is something every mother on this side of Mars would love to see for a change and is very doable for dad and the kids. As far as the dessert is concerned, get her favorite (probably something chocolate) at a bakery. Sure, you can make it from a mix, but I've got you busy here with a full meal. Let's let the pros handle dessert.

So let's do dinner—a maternal meal she'll never forget!

SIMPLE DECORATING FOR MOTHER'S DAY

A cleared-off dinner table is a great start. From there, if you can manage to iron some napkins and throw some candles and a few flowers on the table, you're a hero. The flowers can be picked up the same time you get the groceries. I love supermarket flowers—they're cheap and if you arrange them yourself (cut them and place them in a pretty vase), they can look like they came from a fancy florist. Roses are a good start and are usually pretty cheap.

Here's how to pull this one off. First of all, look for *one* kind of flower instead of an arrangement of all different ones. Those are pretty too, but all roses, for example, is easier to do. Get rid of the baby's breath (you can put the baby's breath in a vase by itself). The fern needs to go, too—it looks too "prom." If they give you lemon leaf, you can use that with the roses, then cut the stems down and place all the roses in a shorter vase—the kind that can go on the dining table so you can see over the top.

Don't forget candles, and the lights should be dimmed or off. This is what sets the mood!

The Menu

SERVES 6

EASY ARTICHOKE SALAD

SKILLET MEDITERRANEAN CHICKEN

PARSLIED RED POTATOES

ASPARAGUS WITH FETA AND LEMON

GLAZED BALSAMIC BABY CARROTS

BAKERY DESSERT (GET MOM'S FAVORITE)

THE SHOPPING LIST

MEAT

6 boneless, skinless chicken breast halves

CONDIMENTS

1 (14-ounce) can/jar artichoke hearts

1 small jar capers

1 jar Kalamata olives (1½ cups)

Olive oil

Balsamic vinegar

White wine (optional)

PRODUCE

1 head romaine lettuce

1 head red leaf lettuce

1 medium red bell pepper

1 medium onion

12 cherry tomatoes

1 pint grape tomatoes (or an additional ½ pint cherry
    tomatoes, if grape not available)

18 small red potatoes

1 bunch parsley

1 pound asparagus

2 lemons

Baby carrots (need 3 cups)

CANNED GOODS

1 (14.5-ounce) can chicken broth (optional)

DAIRY/DAIRY CASE

Butter

1 cup low-fat sour cream

Feta cheese (¼ cup, crumbled)

DRY GOODS

1 (7-ounce) envelope dry Italian salad dressing mix

Brown sugar (1 tablespoon)

Coffee (beans, if you have a grinder)

OTHER

Sandwich-size zipper-topped plastic bags

TOOLS OF THE TRADE

No special tools are required for this simple but elegant dinner for Mom, but a coffee grinder would be a plus to serving a great cup of coffee with that extra-special dessert (see page 155)!

EASY ARTICHOKE SALAD

Serves 6

1 cup low-fat sour cream
1 (7-ounce) envelope dry Italian salad dressing mix
4 cups chopped romaine lettuce
1 cup chopped red bell pepper
¼ cup diced onion
1 (14-ounce) can artichoke hearts, drained and chopped
6 large red leaf lettuce leaves
12 cherry tomatoes

In a small bowl, whisk together the sour cream and dressing mix.

In a large bowl, toss together the remaining ingredients, except the red leaf lettuce and cherry tomatoes. Top with dressing and toss well. Refrigerate your salad until it's time to serve.

To serve, line each plate with a red leaf lettuce leaf, and place a scoop of artichoke salad on top. Garnish with 2 cherry tomatoes on the side and serve.

SKILLET MEDITERRANEAN CHICKEN

Serves 6

> 1 pint grape tomatoes (use halved cherry tomatoes if grape tomatoes
>   aren't available)
> 1½ cups pitted Kalamata olives
> 4 tablespoons capers, rinsed and drained
> 4 tablespoons olive oil
> 6 boneless, skinless chicken breast halves
> Salt and pepper to taste
> ¼–½ cup chicken broth, water, or white wine (if needed; see
>   instructions)

In a medium bowl, toss together the tomatoes, olives, capers, and half the olive oil and set aside.

Season the chicken well with salt and pepper (see page 141). In a large skillet, heat the remaining olive oil over medium-high heat until hot. Add the chicken and cook until nice and golden brown, about 4 minutes on each side. Add the tomato mixture to the skillet, cover, and simmer on low till cooked through, about 8 minutes. Watch it to make sure it isn't sticking. If it is, you can add chicken broth to help it finish cooking and make more of a sauce.

SEASONED WITH SALT AND PEPPER

You will notice in a lot of my recipes, I say "salt and pepper to taste." There is a reason for this—not because I'm trying to frustrate you! Salt should be added slowly and, depending on the recipe, in steps. That's how the pros do it and it makes sense. This is how to get the best taste and to make sure you don't oversalt. The reason to salt anything is to bring out the flavor of food, not mask it.

But salt is salt is salt . . . right? Not necessarily. There is a big difference in types of salt: kosher, sea salt, and regular table salt. You may want to rethink your salt shaker. Kosher salt is coarse and free of any additives. The taste is lighter, less salty than regular table salt and is a good choice for cooking. As a matter of fact, in a poll of 50 top U.S. chefs, 86 percent preferred cooking with kosher salt to any other kind.

Sea salt is made from evaporated seawater and contains the extra minerals found in the seawater itself. Baleine (French for "whale") is the brand of sea salt most readily available in supermarkets. It comes in a blue container with a whale on the label. It's pricier than table salt, for sure, but it will last awhile.

Table salt is pure sodium chloride with a small amount of chemical substance that stops it from clunking together and, therefore, is free flowing. Believe it or not, table salt often has dextrose (a sugar) added to stabilize it—who knew?

Just remember: the flavor of your food is truly worth its salt, especially when you are using a quality salt. But what about the pepper part of the equation?

This is one thing that every kitchen should not be without: a peppermill. Pepper, the freshly ground variety, will do more for a dish than an exotic herb. Why grind, you say? Well for starters, peppercorns have delicate oils in them that are released immediately upon grinding. That's bad news for the pre-ground variety of pepper because by the time it makes it from the can to your shaker and into the dish you're preparing, it's flat, bland, and doesn't offer the punch. With just a flick of the wrist, your soups, salads, entrees, and anything else you're cooking will take on a new dimension. It's truly amazing what freshly ground pepper will do.

That's why annoying waiters all over America can be seen wielding huge peppermills anytime you order a salad. Fresh pepper makes a big difference, no matter what the size of the peppermill.

Source: Adapted from Leanne Ely, *Saving Dinner* (New York: Ballantine Books, 2003).

PARSLIED RED POTATOES

Serves 6

18 small red potatoes, peeled in the center only
2 tablespoons butter
2 tablespoons finely chopped parsley

In a saucepan filled with water, cook the potatoes until tender and then drain.

Add the butter and parsley. Place the lid tightly on the saucepan and shake to mix, then serve 3 potatoes on each plate.

ASPARAGUS WITH FETA AND LEMON

Serves 6

1 pound fresh asparagus spears, woody ends trimmed
¼ cup feta cheese, crumbled
2 lemons, cut into wedges

Bring a large pot of water to a boil. Place the asparagus in the boiling water and cook for about 3 to 5 minutes, depending on how thick the asparagus are. You don't want them overcooked, but cooked till bright green and still crisp-tender.

Drain the asparagus and place on separate dinner plates. Sprinkle feta cheese over the top and serve with a lemon wedge on the side.

GLAZED BALSAMIC BABY CARROTS

Serves 6

1 tablespoon olive oil
3 cups baby carrots
1½ tablespoons balsamic vinegar
1 tablespoon brown sugar

In a skillet over medium-high heat, heat the olive oil. Sauté the carrots in the oil for about 10 minutes, stirring as you go—they will burn if you leave them alone too long. Stir in the vinegar and brown sugar; mix to coat, cover, and let sit for a few minutes (for flavors to meld), then serve.

The Timeline

THREE DAYS AHEAD

If you're going to use a linen tablecloth and napkins, check to see if they need pressing and do it now. They can be folded for later use.

Gather up your candles and candle holders and decide on an arrangement; likewise, a flower container (vase).

A BEAUTIFUL PLATE

The secret to pulling off a wonderful meal is in the timing and presentation. You will notice in the timeline the exact timing for making this meal happen. Follow those instructions; your dinner will not only be done on time and quickly but everything will be hot at the same time.

Once you have cooked everything, serve it beautifully. Let's start with the plate. Pretend it's a clock for a minute so we can get the placement of everything. Place the chicken on first at six o'clock, ladling the sauce carefully over the top. Next, add the potatoes (three per plate) at ten o'clock. Then you want the carrots at twelve o'clock and lastly, the asparagus at two o'clock. Your plate will be lovely. If you mess up with a splash of sauce here or asparagus sliding over there, just stack up the asparagus with clean hands and using a clean cloth, wipe the sauce so the rim of the plate is nice and clean.

There you have it—a restaurant-quality meal, courtesy of Dad and the kids.

Don't forget that one of the big parts to this dinner is cleaning up. Should you follow my cooking instructions, do the flowers the way I tell you, and even iron the napkins and make a spectacular dinner only to leave the dirty dishes for Mom, you might as well buy a one-way ticket for Siberia because it's gonna get cold where you live.

The clean-up is as important as the actual dinner. There are some clever ideas to make this easier than you think. Follow these guidelines for a quick clean-up:

1. Start with a clean kitchen. Make sure the dishwasher is emptied and ready to take on your dinner aftermath.
2. Keep a hot sudsy sink to throw in your pots and pans and miscellaneous stuff you're using while cooking. *Warning:* don't throw cutting knives into sinks filled with billowing suds. That's a surefire way to sever an artery—well, maybe not an artery, but you could cut yourself. Instead, rinse the knives as you use them and set them on the side of the sink for cleaning later.
3. Clean as you go. Keep dipping your cloth into the hot sudsy water and wiping down and cleaning surfaces (the stovetop and counters) as you go.
4. The "put-away" principle. Use what you need, then put away the rest. Remember to do this properly—tightly close the spice jars, close bags of frozen chicken breasts and secure them, placing them back in the freezer, and so on.

Follow these easy steps during the cooking process and you'll have nearly no clean-up at the end.

TWO DAYS AHEAD

Double-check your serving pieces and kitchen utensils. Now is the time to borrow or buy anything you don't have.

ONE DAY AHEAD

Check your shopping list against your pantry and buy everything you need.

Prepare dressing for the Easy Artichoke Salad (page 139); cover and refrigerate.

Chop parsley for Parslied Red Potatoes (page 142); store in a zipper-topped plastic bag and refrigerate.

TWO HOURS AHEAD

Set your table.

Prepare Easy Artichoke Salad and top with refrigerated dressing; cover and refrigerate.

20 MINUTES AHEAD

Prepare Skillet Mediterranean Chicken (page 140).

Cook potatoes.

10 MINUTES AHEAD

Line each salad plate or bowl with a red leaf lettuce leaf and scoop Easy Artichoke Salad on the top; garnish each serving with 2 cherry tomatoes on the side; place on your table.

Sauté the baby carrots . . . don't leave them, or they could burn.

TIME TO EAT!

Finish off the Glazed Balsamic Baby Carrots (page 144).

Finish off the Parslied Red Potatoes (page 142).

Follow the directions from the box called A Beautiful Plate (page 144) so you can arrange the plates skillfully.

Dinner is served!

FATHER'S DAY

How often do you hear about Dad getting breakfast in bed? On weekend mornings, he's the guy who is up and at 'em sooner than anyone doing household chores and fix-it stuff. While Mom and the kids sleep in, he's the guy pushing the lawn mower, schlepping to the hardware store, and cleaning out the garage—at least that's how I imagine it to be. How about a day of full-on pampering for Dad on his day of days, starting with a man-size breakfast in bed? That ought to make him feel like King of his Castle!

The Menu SERVES 6

CLASSIC BELGIAN WAFFLES

MAKIN' BACON

FLUFFY SCRAMBLED EGGS

HONEYDEW AND BLUEBERRIES

FRESHLY SQUEEZED OJ

THE SHOPPING LIST

MEAT

1 pound center-cut thick bacon

CONDIMENTS

Vegetable oil

PRODUCE

1 large ripe honeydew melon

1 pint blueberries

1 orange (if freshly squeezed orange juice not available)

SPICES

Vanilla extract

DAIRY/DAIRY CASE

Unsalted butter (¾ cup plus 1 tablespoon)

Milk (3⅓ cups)

Eggs (15)

Freshly squeezed orange juice

DRY GOODS

1 (2.5-ounce) package active dry yeast

Sugar

Real maple syrup

Unbleached all-purpose flour

Coffee (beans, if you have a grinder)

OTHER

Gallon-size zipper-topped plastic bags

Aluminum foil wrap

Plastic wrap

TOOLS OF THE TRADE

Waffle iron (you need a Belgian waffle iron, this is bigger
    than the standard waffle iron)

Pastry brush

9 × 13-inch baking pan

Jelly-roll pan

Electric mixer

Wire whisk

Coffee grinder (optional)

Breakfast tray (this *is* breakfast in bed, after all!)

CLASSIC BELGIAN WAFFLES

Serves 6

1 (2.5-ounce) package active dry yeast
3 cups warm milk (about 110 degrees)
3 egg yolks
¾ cup unsalted butter, melted and cooled to lukewarm
½ cup sugar
Pinch of salt
2 teaspoons vanilla extract
4 cups unbleached all-purpose flour
3 egg whites
Vegetable oil, for brushing waffle iron

In a small bowl, dissolve the yeast in ¼ cup of the warm milk. Mix and let stand until slightly bubbly, about 10 minutes.

Meanwhile, in a large bowl, whisk together the egg yolks, ¼ cup of warm milk, and the melted butter. Now add in the yeast mixture, then the sugar, salt, and vanilla. Add the remaining 2½ cups milk, mixing alternately with the flour.

In another bowl, beat the egg whites until they reach soft peaks. Carefully fold your beaten egg whites into the batter. Cover the bowl tightly with plastic wrap, and let rise in a warm place until doubled in volume, about 2 hours.

When it's about 15 minutes away from waffle time, preheat the waffle iron. When you're ready to make your first waffle, brush the waffle iron lightly with oil (using a pastry brush), making sure you get every crevice, then spoon about ½ cup (or as recommended by waffle maker's manufacturer) into the center of the waffle iron. Close the lid and bake until it stops steaming and the waffle is golden brown. Serve immediately or keep warm till serving time in a warm oven. Don't stack the waffles though; they will get soggy and mushy; instead, put them in a 9 × 13-inch pan, spread out, in a 250 degree oven.

Serve with butter and real maple syrup.

MAKIN' BACON

Cooking bacon can be a greasy, messy experience, especially when you're doing it on the stovetop in a skillet. The solution? Cook it in the oven.

First, you need a jelly-roll pan. People sometimes mistakenly call jelly-roll pans cookie sheets. Cookie sheets have no sides; jelly-roll pans do, with a rim of about ¾-inch. Don't make the mistake of doing the bacon on a cookie sheet or you will have a grease fire in your oven.

1 pound center-cut thick bacon

Preheat the oven to 400 degrees.

Line a jelly-roll pan with foil and then arrange the bacon slices on the foil, side by side. Cook the bacon for about 5 to 10 minutes, depending on the thickness of the bacon. Make sure you've placed your pan in the middle of the oven for even cooking. Check on it midway to see if it's cooking evenly. If it's not, you will need to turn the pan to get it evenly cooked.

Once the bacon is cooked to your liking, remove the pan carefully from the oven. Use tongs to remove the bacon from the greasy pan and place the cooked pieces of bacon on a paper towel–lined plate to drain. Now leave your pan to cool. Keep the bacon wrapped in paper towels and zap in the microwave just before serving.

NOTE: The foil is a great trick because once the bacon grease congeals on the pan after cooking, you can roll the whole mess up and toss it. No need to pour off the hot bacon grease.

FLUFFY SCRAMBLED EGGS

Serves 6

It's easy to muff up scrambled eggs. They may be a simple thing to make, but making them fluffy and just right takes some finesse.

> *12 eggs*
> *⅓ cup milk*
> *Salt and pepper to taste*
> *1 tablespoon unsalted butter*

Crack the eggs into a large bowl. Be careful not to get any shell in there. Using a wire whisk, heartily beat the eggs till well mixed and frothy. Add the milk and salt and pepper.

In a nonstick skillet over medium-high heat, melt the butter. Spread the butter around in the pan with your plastic spatula, and then add the eggs. Let the eggs sit just a minute and watch for them to start to set. This is the key to good eggs. Now, using the same spatula, push the eggs toward the center of the pan, lifting the set stuff and allowing the wet stuff to get next to the pan. This sounds strange, I know, but this is how I was taught when I worked as a cook in a coffee shop. (I also learned to crack eggs with one hand and could flip eggs in a pan to turn them—nifty party tricks.) This technique really does make the best scrambled eggs. They're not too runny, too hard, or overscrambled.

HONEYDEW AND BLUEBERRIES

Serves 6

1 large ripe honeydew melon
1 pint fresh blueberries, washed

Cut the honeydew into wedges. It would be great if you could get 6 wedges per half from the melon. Take the skin off the wedges. Then on your plate, place 2 wedges on their side and sprinkle a handful of blueberries over the top. The color contrast is beautiful, and these two fruits are a wonderful match. See how simple this is?

FRESHLY SQUEEZED OJ

What? Did you really think I'd have you squeezing fresh orange juice first thing in the morning? You can buy it that way, so don't bother.

If you can't get freshly squeezed OJ, then squeeze one orange into a glass and add regular old OJ to it. A quick stir with a fork and you're ready to go.

JAVA JIVE

If there is one thing I must have every morning, it's a cup of coffee. Good coffee, not the swill you get from those huge barrels at gas stations. Real coffee, freshly ground, freshly brewed, the whole bit.

If your coffee knowledge is limited, now is the time to bean up on how it's done so you can give dear old Dad a cuppa joe he'll never forget.

- A clean machine. If your coffeemaker is dirty, your coffee is going to be nasty. Look at the instructions the manufacturer gave you to clean it properly. You may need to demineralize it, too. That involves flushing out the mechanism with a tablespoon of white vinegar and a pot of clean water, and brewing it, followed by brewing a clean pot of water. This will help to decalcify the inner workings of the coffeemaker. But before you take on this project, check the owner's manual. Not all coffeemakers need this or should have this type of treatment.

- Cold water. Use fresh cold water for each pot. I generally let my tap run for a couple of minutes before putting the pot under it. That way, the pipes are cleared and the water is fresh and new. If your tapwater is full of minerals, you may want to consider using bottled water for your coffee.

- Measure. The general rule of measurement for coffee making is 1 heaping tablespoon ground coffee per 1 cup water. I use a little more than that because I like it stronger.

- Grind it. I hate to saddle you with another piece of equipment, but there really is no comparison to freshly ground coffee. A coffee mill will set you back about fifteen bucks. Pop for it. This is a good investment.

- Coffee storage. Coffee sitting on a burner in a glass carafe for more than fifteen minutes is going to taste burned. Store it in a thermal carafe right after making it and it will be good up to an hour after brewing.

The Timeline

TWO DAYS AHEAD

Check your kitchen equipment to see what items you may have to buy or borrow.

Plan your Breakfast in Bed presentation (tray, placemat, napkin, etc.).

ONE DAY AHEAD

Check your shopping list against your pantry and buy all items you need.

TWO AND A HALF HOURS AHEAD

Prepare batter for Classic Belgian Waffles (page 151) and set aside in a warm place, according to recipe directions.

ONE HOUR AHEAD

Rinse and drain blueberries; place in a large zipper-topped plastic bag; refrigerate.

Slice honeydew melon into 12 wedges; peel and place in a large zipper-topped plastic bag; refrigerate.

FIFTEEN MINUTES AHEAD

Preheat the oven to 400 degrees (for bacon).

Preheat the waffle iron.

Prepare Fluffy Scrambled Eggs mixture.

Ready your coffee to the point of pushing the "go" button.

TEN MINUTES AHEAD

Cook Makin' Bacon (page 152).

Cook Classic Belgian Waffles (page 151).

Pour Freshly Squeezed OJ (page 153).

Push the "go" button on the coffeemaker.

Check on the bacon and follow recipe directions.

FIVE MINUTES AHEAD

Cook Fluffy Scrambled Eggs (page 153).

Assemble breakfast tray and serve!

GRADUATION

Graduation is a celebration that usually ends up with your graduate taking off with friends to celebrate this milestone. To that end, a full-on dinner party might not pass muster, and squeezing in a celebration with some fun desserts and coffee might be just the ticket before your grad launches off to other parties with his fellow alums.

The key to pulling off this party is the plan-ahead factor: all the desserts were done ahead of time with none requiring anything last-minute, like whipping cream or assembling many-layered cakes. It's all easy, fast, and delicious, with a little help from a few mixes! There is no written or implied rule anywhere that says in order to entertain properly you must break your neck, stress yourself out, and make everything from scratch. Martha Stewart did that and ended up in jail. Well, maybe not for those reasons, but if I had to do everything from absolute scratch, I would end up in jail for disturbing the peace, at the very least.

◆ The Menu

SHORTCUT BROWNIES

MARVELOUS MAGIC BARS

SNICKERS CHEESECAKE

UNDERHANDED LEMON BARS

EASY SUMMER FRUIT CRISP

CHOCOLATE-COVERED STRAWBERRIES

THE SHOPPING LIST

CONDIMENTS
Vegetable oil

PRODUCE
1 lemon

Peaches (1 cup, sliced)

Apples (1 cup, sliced)

Pears (1 cup, sliced)

1 cup blueberries

1 cup raspberries

2 cups strawberries

24 large strawberries with leaves (or stems, if available)

CANNED GOODS
1 (14-ounce) can sweetened condensed milk

SPICES
Vanilla extract

DAIRY/DAIRY CASE
Butter (1 cup)

Milk (¼ cup, and see mix instructions)

4 eggs
3 (8-ounce) packages cream cheese

DRY GOODS
1 package brownie mix—your favorite
2 boxes lemon bar mix
1 (16-ounce) package semisweet chocolate chips
1 (12-ounce) package semisweet chocolate morsels
Confectioners' sugar (1 cup)
Graham cracker crumbs (2¾ cups)
Flaked coconut (1⅓ cups)
Chopped nuts (1 cup)
Sugar
Unbleached all-purpose flour
Oatmeal (⅓ cup)
Baking powder

FROZEN FOODS
Vanilla ice cream

OTHER
Quart-size zipper-topped plastic bags
Plastic wrap
Waxed paper
2 (2.16-ounce) Snickers bars
Toothpicks

TOOLS OF THE TRADE
9-inch springform cake pan
Double boiler
9 × 13-inch baking pan
3-quart baking dish

SHORTCUT BROWNIES

Makes 24 brownies

1 package of brownie mix (I like Betty Crocker's)
1 (8-ounce) package semisweet chocolate chips
⅓ cup confectioners' sugar

This is easy. All you have to do is follow the instructions on the package of brownies. Sprinkle the chocolate chips on top and bake. (I prefer them on top as opposed to being mixed in because the brownies become too gooey. Yes, there is such a thing as a too-gooey brownie. When they're perched on top, they still goo up a bit, but the texture is so much better and they look nice and bumpy on top.) When your brownies have sufficiently cooled and you've cut them evenly (for this event, it would be a good idea to cut them smaller, more bite-size), dump the confectioners' sugar into a wire-mesh handheld sieve, and sprinkle the sugar over the top. Make sure you've already cooled and cut the brownies, though. Otherwise the sugar will get all gooped up and become a big mess.

MARVELOUS MAGIC BARS

Makes 24 bars

½ cup butter
1½ cups graham cracker crumbs
1 (14-ounce) can sweetened condensed milk
1 (12-ounce) package semisweet chocolate morsels
1⅓ cups flaked coconut
1 cup chopped nuts

Preheat the oven to 350 degrees.

In 9 × 13-inch baking pan, melt the butter in the oven. Sprinkle the graham cracker crumbs over the melted butter; then pour the condensed milk evenly over the crumbs. Layer evenly with remaining ingredients; press down firmly.

Bake for 25 minutes or until golden brown. Let cool, then cut into bars.

SNICKERS CHEESECAKE

Serves 12

3 tablespoons unsalted butter, melted
1¼ cups graham cracker crumbs
¾ cup plus 1 tablespoon sugar
3 (8-ounce) packages cream cheese, at room temperature
3 eggs
2 teaspoons vanilla extract
2 (2.16-ounce) Snickers bars, chopped

Preheat the oven to 350 degrees.

In a small bowl, combine the butter, graham cracker crumbs, and 1 tablespoon sugar.

Press into the bottom of a 9-inch springform pan. Bake for 10 minutes, then set aside to cool briefly. Keep the oven on.

Meanwhile, in a large bowl, cream the remaining sugar and the cream cheese together until smooth. Add the eggs, one at a time, and the vanilla. Stir in the chopped candy bar (and try not to eat it!), and pour into the baked crust.

Bake for 45 minutes. Let it cool, then refrigerate for at least 3 hours. Carefully remove the pan, and slice and serve!

UNDERHANDED LEMON BARS

Makes 12 bars

Here's another un-recipe, much like the Shortcut Brownies. This trick came from my best friend Sharon Johnston, who learned it from Linda Giannini. Good stuff like this travels quickly from friend to friend. Now I'm telling you—you can tell a friend, too, if you like.

> *2 boxes lemon bar mix*
> *1 fresh lemon, zest grated*
> *½ cup confectioners' sugar*

Just follow the simple instructions on the boxes of this mix. When you get to the lemon filling part, add 1 teaspoon per box of fresh lemon zest (see page 113).

When the pan has cooled, cut into bars. Use your wire-mesh hand-held sieve to sprinkle confectioners' sugar over the top. Place the lemon bars on a footed serving dish, add a sprig of lemon leaf, and you've got a dessert that is worthy of a magazine cover.

EASY SUMMER FRUIT CRISP

Serves 12

Even though apples and pears aren't exactly summer fruits, their heartiness helps the crisp stand up a little bit more.

1 cup peeled and sliced peach
1 cup peeled, cored, and sliced apple
1 cup peeled, cored, and sliced pear
1 cup blueberries
1 cup raspberries
2 cups strawberries
1 egg
¾ cup sugar
¼ cup milk
1 cup unbleached all-purpose flour
1 teaspoon baking powder
½ teaspoon salt
⅓ cup oatmeal
½ teaspoon vanilla extract
2 tablespoons butter, melted
Vanilla ice cream

Preheat the oven to 350 degrees. Lightly grease a 3-quart baking dish.

In a bowl, toss together carefully all the fruit, then layer it on the bottom of your baking dish. In a large bowl, beat the egg with the sugar and milk. In yet another bowl, sift together the flour, baking powder, and salt; stir in the oatmeal, then add this to the egg mixture. Stir in the vanilla and melted butter, then spoon batter on top of the fruit.

Bake for about 30 minutes or until the crisp is golden brown and bubbling. Serve warm with vanilla ice cream.

CHOCOLATE-COVERED STRAWBERRIES

Makes 24 berries

1 (8-ounce) package semisweet chocolate chips
1 teaspoon vegetable oil
24 large strawberries with leaves (or stems, if available)

Melt the chocolate and oil in a double boiler; stirring until smooth.

Partially dip each strawberry in the chocolate mixture, then place on a waxed paper–lined baking sheet. Allow to harden for about 1 hour.

The Timeline

TWO WEEKS AHEAD

Have your graduate send out invitations.

ONE WEEK AHEAD

Check your serving pieces and kitchen tools against the recipe directions and buy or borrow anything you'll need.

If using a linen tablecloth, does it need pressing? Do it now and hang or fold it for later.

THREE DAYS AHEAD

Clean out your refrigerator.

Check your pantry against the shopping list and head for the grocery store. Buy everything you need *except* the fruit.

TWO DAYS AHEAD

Bake the Shortcut Brownies (page 161), Marvelous Magic Bars (page 162), and Underhanded Lemon Bars (page 164); cool completely, slice, cover with plastic wrap, and store in refrigerator.

ONE DAY AHEAD

Shop for the fruit listed in the produce section of the Shopping List.

Rinse and drain berries; store in separate zipper-topped plastic bags in the refrigerator.

Bake the Snickers Cheesecake (page 163); completely cool, then remove from the springform pan to your serving platter; stick a few toothpicks in the top and cover with plastic wrap; refrigerate.

ONE HOUR AHEAD

Prepare and bake the Easy Summer Fruit Crisp (page 165).

Remove Shortcut Brownies, Marvelous Magic Bars, and Under-handed Lemon Bars from refrigerator; arrange on serving platters or trays.

Remove the Snickers Cheesecake from refrigerator and slice. Prepare Chocolate-Covered Strawberries (page 166); arrange on serving platter or tray; refrigerate.

ONE-HALF HOUR AHEAD

Check on Easy Summer Fruit Crisp; if done, remove from oven.

FIFTEEN MINUTES AHEAD

Check to make sure everything is out and ready—enjoy!

FOURTH OF JULY

This is one holiday that demands barbecue, barbecue, and more barbecue. Is there any other option on a hot and sticky summer day? You won't catch me turning on the oven anytime soon! So let's keep the heat outdoors where it belongs and crank up the barby to full throttle and give it a workout, shall we? Off we go to the barbecue!

INDEPENDENT DECORATING

If you have a large red-and-white checkered tablecloth for your buffet, you're halfway there. Use a blue ribbon to tie the silverware in the napkin and place in a basket. Consider a small vase of bachelor's buttons or another pretty blue flower—you don't want great big flower arrangements. Stick a couple of small flags in the flowers, place some votives on the table, and you have a distinctly lovely table without the fuss. The point is to keep it simple. Let the food do the talking and the decorating be a mere accessory.

The Menu

ASIAN COLESLAW WITH PEANUTS AND CILANTRO

GRILLED POTATO SALAD WITH ROSEMARY
   MAYONNAISE

GRILLED ALE'D BRATWURST

CONFETTI CORN RELISH

GRILLED TERIYAKI CHICKEN

SUNDAE BAR

THE SHOPPING LIST

MEAT
8 bratwurst sausages
8 boneless, skinless chicken breast halves

CONDIMENTS
Vegetable oil
Roasted sesame oil
Cider vinegar
Rice wine vinegar
Soy sauce (low-sodium, if available)
Teriyaki sauce
Mayonnaise
Tabasco
Honey
1 bottle chocolate sauce
1 bottle caramel sauce
2 jars maraschino cherries

PRODUCE
1 bag coleslaw mix
1 bag broccoli slaw mix

1 small red onion

3 white onions

1 head garlic

1 large red bell pepper

1 bunch green onions

1 bunch cilantro

3 pounds potatoes

1 bunch ripe bananas

2 quarts strawberries

SPICES

Rosemary

Black peppercorns

Ground cumin

DAIRY/DAIRY CASE

Buttermilk (¼ cup)

2 to 3 cans real whipped cream

DRY GOODS

Sugar

Dry-roasted peanuts

Chopped nuts (for ice cream sundaes)

Chocolate chips

Butterscotch chips

FROZEN FOODS

3 (10-ounce) packages corn kernels

1 gallon vanilla ice cream

1 gallon chocolate ice cream

1 gallon strawberry ice cream

BAKERY

8 submarine or hoagie rolls

OTHER

4 bottles dark ale

M & M's

Gallon-size zipper-topped plastic bags

Charcoal or mesquite

Charcoal lighter or lighter fluid

TOOLS OF THE TRADE

Large barbecue

Barbecue tools

Pastry brush

Ice cream scoop

The Recipes

ASIAN COLESLAW WITH PEANUTS AND CILANTRO

Serves 8

1 bag broccoli slaw mix
1 bag coleslaw mix
1 small red onion, finely chopped
⅓ cup rice wine vinegar
1 tablespoon light soy sauce
1 teaspoon sugar
1 teaspoon vegetable oil
1 teaspoon roasted sesame oil
¼ cup coarsely chopped cilantro, plus more for garnish
⅓ cup dry-roasted peanuts, coarsely chopped, plus more for garnish

In a large bowl, combine the bagged mixes and onion; toss well.

In a small bowl, whisk together the vinegar, soy sauce, and sugar. Whisking constantly, drizzle in both oils. Continue to whisk until thickened.

Add the dressing and the cilantro and peanuts to the cabbage/ broccoli slaw mixture and toss thoroughly. Refrigerate for a little while or serve right away (better to let flavors meld). Before serving, toss one more time and sprinkle the top with the additional cilantro and peanuts.

GRILLED POTATO SALAD WITH
ROSEMARY MAYONNAISE

Serves 8

3 pounds potatoes, peeled, cut in half lengthwise, and parboiled
1–2 tablespoons vegetable oil
½ cup mayonnaise
¼ cup buttermilk
½ cup cider vinegar
1 tablespoon sugar
1 tablespoon crushed rosemary
2 teaspoons salt
Ground black pepper to taste
½ cup chopped onion

Fire up the barby to preheat.

Bring a large pot of salted water to a boil. Add the potatoes and cook until tender but still firm, about 10 minutes. Drain and let cool.

Using a pastry brush, lightly brush the potatoes on all sides with oil. Grill the potatoes to mark them, then allow to cool again. When cool, carefully dice them.

In a large bowl, whisk together the mayo, buttermilk, vinegar, sugar, rosemary, salt, and pepper. Gently stir in the potatoes and onion. Let stand for 1 hour before serving so flavors have a chance to meld.

YOU GRILL, GIRL!

Just because you're not a guy doesn't mean you can't yank out the barby and fire it up with the best of them! Grilling is like cooking anything . . . sort of.

Only outdoors.

Before you end up any more confused, here are a few tips gleaned here and there that will help you grill beautifully instead of char mercilessly. Subtle changes in temperatures can mean the difference between dinner and shoe leather, so study up before you fire it up!

- Make it clean. Dirty grills are going to leave dirty schmootz on your qu'ed food. Avoid this by always cleaning the grill after you use it and while it's still relatively warm.
- Stoke the fire. Use only plain old charcoal or mesquite. Using that ready-to-light stuff tastes like you cooked your hamburgers over a Bic lighter. Take your time and use the real thing.
- Cool tools. Using regular kitchen tongs to turn your chicken could prove hazardous to your health. The handles aren't long enough, and you may end up burned. Use real BBQ tools.
- Feel the burn. Most barbecues aren't equipped with thermometers. So how do you know when the grill is ready? Hold your hand, palm side down, about 6 inches from the grill and count (one Mississippi, two Mississippi . . .) until the heat is uncomfortable and you have to pull your hand away. Here are the guidelines:

    Two seconds—it's hot, about 375 degrees
    Three seconds—it's medium-hot, about 350 or so degrees
    Four seconds—it's medium, about 300 degrees, give or take
    Five seconds—it's low, probably closer to 200, maybe a few degrees more

- Timing is everything. Grilling time is going to vary according to what you're cooking, the thickness of the food, and the heat of the grill. Make sure you have enough time to get your fire just right.
- Cut the fat. To avoid grease fires, trim all visible fat from your meat.
- Smoking section. To enjoy the smoky flavor of wood chips without the mess, soak a handful of wood chips in water for 30 minutes and wrap in a foil pouch. Pierce the pouch with a fork to release the smoke and place directly on the coals. The chips will smoke away and not flame up.
- Put a lid on it. You'll lose a lot of valuable heat if you keep opening and closing the grill lid. If the temperature is right, simply turn your food once and close it back up.
- Sweet and saucy. Barbecue sauces should be added toward the end of cooking or they will just burn right off. Marinades, however, are inside the meat and aren't a problem.
- Veg out. To keep your veggies from drying out over an open flame, soak them in water for half an hour before grilling. Then lightly brush them with olive oil for flavor and so they won't stick to the grill.

GRILLED ALE'D BRATWURST

Serves 8

4 bottles dark ale
4 cups water
8 bratwurst sausages, pricked with a fork
1½ cups thinly sliced onions
8 sub or hoagie rolls

In a large saucepan, combine the ale and water over high heat. Bring the ale mixture to a boil and add the bratwurst. Turn down the heat and simmer for about 15 minutes.

In the meantime, fire up the barby and let that thing get hot, about medium-high heat. Make sure your grate is clean and lightly oiled.

Barbecue your bratwurst for about 10 minutes, turning occasionally to brown evenly. Serve hot off the grill with the onions and Confetti Corn Relish (page 178) on the rolls.

CONFETTI CORN RELISH

Serves 8

1 large red bell pepper
¼ cup cider vinegar
2 tablespoons honey
1–2 teaspoons Tabasco
2 teaspoons ground cumin
Salt and pepper to taste
⅓ cup vegetable oil
3 (10-ounce) packages frozen corn kernels, thawed and drained
½ cup chopped green onion

Roast the red pepper over a gas flame or under the broiler until blackened on all sides. Remove from heat and seal in a plastic zipper-topped bag and let sit for 10 minutes or till sweating. The peel will come off easily now; peel, seed, and chop.

In a large bowl, combine the vinegar, honey, Tabasco, cumin, and salt and pepper. Gradually whisk in the oil. Add the chopped red pepper, corn, and green onion. Mix well. Cover and refrigerate overnight, stirring occasionally.

This relish can be made up to 2 days ahead of time. Let stand at room temperature for 30 minutes before serving.

GRILLED TERIYAKI CHICKEN

Serves 8

8 boneless, skinless chicken breast halves
2 cups bottled teriyaki sauce (I like Kikkoman)
½ cup rice wine vinegar
8 garlic cloves, pressed
1 tablespoon roasted sesame oil

In a large zipper-topped bag, combine the ingredients and smush all around to coat evenly. Let the chicken marinate in the fridge for at least 4 hours.

Make sure your grill is clean and lightly oiled. Fire up the barbecue to medium-high heat.

Place the chicken on the grill and cook 6 to 8 minutes on each side, till cooked through.

SUNDAE BAR

Serves 8

> 3 gallons assorted ice cream: chocolate, vanilla, and strawberry or
> your favorites
> 1 bottle chocolate sauce
> 1 bottle caramel sauce
> 2 quarts fresh strawberries, sliced, sprinkled with a little sugar, and
> mixed well
> 1 bunch ripe bananas, peeled and sliced
> 2–3 cans real whipped cream
> 2 cups chopped nuts
> Chocolate chips
> Butterscotch chips
> M & M's
> Anything else you can think of and would like on your sundaes
> 2 jars maraschino cherries

This is really easy. Just put everything out, and let everyone dig in and build his or her own sundae. Put the ice cream out first to soften, while you're setting everything else up. Put the bowls at the beginning of the sundae bar and napkins and spoons at the end, to make it easy.

The Timeline

TEN DAYS AHEAD

Invite your guests.

Check to see if you have all the tools required for the barbecue. If you plan to eat outdoors, do you have enough tables and chairs for all of your guests? If not, now is the time to buy or borrow what you'll need.

TWO DAYS AHEAD

Clean out your refrigerator.

Check your pantry against the shopping list and head for the grocery store.

Prepare Confetti Corn Relish (page 178); cover and refrigerate.

ONE DAY AHEAD

Proceed with the first step of the directions for Grilled Potato Salad with Rosemary Mayonnaise (page 175), place grilled and cooled, diced potatoes in a large zipper-topped plastic bag and refrigerate. Prepare dressing; cover and refrigerate.

OVERNIGHT

Marinate the chicken for Grilled Teriyaki Chicken (page 179); store in refrigerator.

ONE HOUR AHEAD

Prepare Asian Coleslaw with Peanuts and Cilantro (page 174); cover and refrigerate.

ONE-HALF HOUR AHEAD

Pull the Confetti Corn Relish from refrigerator and bring to room temperature.

Thinly slice onions for the Grilled Ale'd Bratwurst (page 177); place in a zipper-topped plastic bag and refrigerate. Chop onions for Grilled Potato Salad with Rosemary Mayonnaise; place in a zipper-topped plastic bag and refrigerate.

Proceed with the last step of the recipe directions for Grilled Potato Salad with Rosemary Mayonnaise, adding diced onions and potatoes to dressing; let stand at room temperature.

Slowly bring water and ale to a boil in a large saucepan for the Grilled Ale'd Bratwurst.

FIFTEEN MINUTES AHEAD

Add the bratwurst sausages to the water and ale mixture and simmer.

Pull the marinated chicken from the refrigerator.

Fire up the barby!

Slice the submarine or hoagie rolls in half and place in a large, napkin-lined basket.

Toss the Asian Coleslaw with Peanuts and Cilantro one more time and garnish with additional cilantro and peanuts.

Arrange all prepared menu items on serving platters/trays.

Happy Fourth of July!

HALLOWEEN

O h, the fun and games that Halloween brings—trick or treat indeed! Having something warm in your tummy before marauding in the streets scavenging for candy is what this little party is all about. The menu here—replete with gross-out names—is guaranteed to get the kids giggling and the adults scarfing. Let the fun begin!

The Menu

CHOCOLATE-COVERED SPIDERS

BARBECUED BAT WINGS

CHOPPED LIZARD SANDWICHES

CARTILAGE AND BLOOD-CLOT SALAD

BLOODY EYEBALLS IN GREEN SLIME

DIRT AND WORM CUPCAKES

KANDI'S KITTY LITTER CAKE

DISMEMBERED-HAND PUNCH

THE SHOPPING LIST

MEAT

4 pounds chicken wings

Chicken meat, cooked (2 cups, chopped)

CONDIMENTS

1 (12-ounce) bottle chili sauce

Salsa—your favorite (2 tablespoons)

Molasses (2 tablespoons)

Worcestershire sauce (2 tablespoons)

1 (16-ounce) bottle coleslaw dressing

Mayonnaise

Sweet pickle relish (1 teaspoon)

Vegetable oil

PRODUCE

2 lemons

Celery (need ½ stalk)

1 bunch green onions

2 (16-ounce) packages broccoli slaw mix

1 bunch red grapes (about 24)
1 huge pumpkin

SPICES
Chili powder
Garlic powder
Ground cumin

DAIRY/DAIRY CASE
Eggs (see mix instructions)
Milk (see mix instructions)

DRY GOODS
1 (8-ounce) package dried cranberries
1 large package lime gelatin
2 large boxes instant vanilla pudding mix
1 chocolate cake mix
2 German chocolate cake mixes
1 (12-ounce) container prepared chocolate icing
1 bag chocolate wafer crumbs
1 box Nilla Wafers
1 (13-ounce) envelope unsweetened grape soft drink mix
1 (13-ounce) envelope unsweetened orange soft drink mix
Sugar
1 (12-ounce) bag semisweet chocolate chips
1 (8.5-ounce) package chow mein noodles

BAKERY
2 loaves party bread—your choice (rye, white, or wheat)

OTHER
1 bag gummy worms
1 bag Tootsie Rolls

Green food coloring

1 liter ginger ale

Cupcake liners

Gallon-size zipper-topped plastic bags

Plastic wrap

2 latex gloves (no powder inside)

Dry ice

1 new cat litter box (without domed lid)

1 new Pooper Scooper

TOOLS OF THE TRADE

Double boiler

Roasting pan

Crock-Pot

Electric mixer

Wire rack

Newspaper pages

1 large punch bowl

9 × 13-inch baking pans (2)

The Recipes

CHOCOLATE-COVERED SPIDERS

Serves 8

1 (12-ounce) bag semisweet chocolate chips
1 (8.5-ounce) package chow mein noodles

Using a double boiler, heat the chocolate chips till melted or place the chocolate chips in a stainless bowl over a pot of simmering water and improvise your own double boiler. Cook, stirring occasionally, until melted and smooth.

Remove chocolate from heat and stir in the chow mein noodles to evenly distribute. Using a soup spoon, spoon out large spoonfuls onto waxed paper. Let cool completely before serving or storing them (you can make these up to 2 days ahead; just store in large zipper-topped bags).

BARBECUED BAT WINGS

Serves 8

4 pounds chicken wings, leave the tips on
1 (12-ounce) bottle chili sauce
¼ cup lemon juice
2 tablespoons molasses
2 tablespoons Worcestershire sauce
2 tablespoons salsa (your favorite)
2 teaspoons chili powder
1 teaspoon garlic powder
1 teaspoon ground cumin
Salt and pepper to taste

Place the chicken in a Crock-Pot.

In a medium bowl, combine the remaining ingredients. Mix and pour over chicken. Cook on high for about 5 hours. (Remember, your Crock-Pot can vary in cooking time because of the size, age, and brand.)

CHOPPED LIZARD SANDWICHES

Makes 12 sandwiches

2 cups cooked and chopped chicken
2 tablespoons mayonnaise
1 teaspoon sweet pickle relish
½ celery stalk, finely chopped
2 green onions, finely chopped (white and a little green)
Salt and pepper to taste
2 loaves party bread (rye, white, or wheat)

In a large bowl, mix the chicken with the mayonnaise, relish, celery, and green onions. Season with salt and pepper. Make up your little sandwiches and cut on the diagonal. You will have enough for about a dozen little sandwiches, maybe a few more. After all, one can only eat so much chopped lizard.

Wrap with plastic and chill until serving time.

CARTILAGE AND BLOOD-CLOT SALAD

Serves 8

2 (16-ounce) packages broccoli slaw mix
1 (16-ounce) bottle coleslaw dressing
1 (8-ounce) package dried cranberries
Salt and pepper to taste

In a large bowl, combine the broccoli slaw, dressing (use more or less depending on your taste), cranberries, and salt and pepper. Mix well, cover, and refrigerate until ready to serve.

BLOODY EYEBALLS IN GREEN SLIME

Serves 8

1 large package lime gelatin
24 or so red grapes, peeled

Peeling the grapes is going to take some time, so first make the lime gelatin according to package ingredients. While you're peeling the grapes, the gelatin can be setting in the fridge. But you don't want it to set all the way; you want it halfway set so it's a wonderfully gelatinous, disgusting mess.

When the gelatin is nearly set and perfectly revolting, add the "eyeballs" (peeled grapes). Mix slightly and serve in a large serving bowl.

DIRT AND WORM CUPCAKES

Makes 12 cupcakes

This is a cinch to make. Let your kids do it—they'll love it!

> 1 chocolate cake mix
> Cupcake liners
> 1 bag chocolate wafer crumbles
> 1 (12-ounce) container prepared chocolate icing
> 1 bag gummy worms

Preheat the oven to 350 degrees.

Prepare the cake mix according to package instructions. Bake the cupcakes in a muffin tin using paper cupcake liners. Allow to cool on a wire rack.

Pour the chocolate wafer crumbles into a pie plate. Ice the cupcakes with the chocolate icing, then gently roll in the crumbles till they're all dipped. Now take the remaining crumbles and pour them evenly on top of the cupcakes, so it looks like potting soil is heaped on top of them. Carefully, weave the gummy worms into the crumbs so they look like earthworms trying to get out of the ground. That's all there is to it!

KANDI'S KITTY LITTER CAKE

Serves 8 (generously)

2 German chocolate cake mixes
2 large boxes vanilla instant pudding mix
1 box Nilla Wafers
Green food coloring
1 bag Tootsie Rolls

1 new cat litter pan—the plain-Jane kind without the
   domed lid
1 new Pooper Scooper
A few pages from your local newspaper

Preheat the oven to 350 degrees.

Prepare the cake mixes and bake according to package directions in 9 × 13-inch pans. Allow the cakes to cool to room temperature.

Prepare the pudding mix and refrigerate until needed.

Process the cookies in small batches in a food processor, scraping often, or put the cookies in a large zipper-topped plastic bag, take out your rolling pin, and beat the cookies. You want crumbles that resemble cat litter. Don't overprocess cookies into a fine powder.

Add a couple drops green food coloring and mix. Repeat the process. You are not trying to totally and completely color the cookies. The cookies should look like gray and green clumps—this is supposed to resemble the chlorophyll in cat litter. Set aside about ¼ cup of this mixture for later.

Once the cakes are cool, crumble them into a large mixing bowl. Toss in half the cookie crumbs and the chilled pudding. Add just enough pudding to moisten the crumbs.

Wash your cat litter pan and Pooper Scooper. (I wash the inside very well, but I've been careful not to get the outside of the pan too wet while cleaning. I've left the stickers on the outside of the pan for a nice effect. I want to make sure everyone knows they are eating from a cat litter pan.) Now put the cake and pudding mixture into the litter box.

Don't forget to pick up a kitty litter pan (yes, a real one) and a kitty litter spoon (also real) to serve your Kitty Litter Cake in. Nothing says lovin' better than Kitty Litter Cake right from the oven, but it's not the same without the full effect of the pan and Pooper Scooper. Kandi Speegle, my assistant, is a regular Kitty Litter Cake baker, and I've included her recipe for this crass confection. She says to really do it up, you need to put the cake on newspaper (in its pan, of course) and make sure the kitty cat "leavings" are appropriately shaped and left "naturally" as any self-respecting kitty cat would do.

So have fun with this—it's the perfect gross-out complement to your hideous Halloween buffet.

Start making cat droppings out of the Tootsie Rolls. Start with about 5 unwrapped rolls on a microwave-safe dish and nuke until soft and pliable, about 10 seconds.

This next part is not for the squeamish, so you may want to get your kids involved at this point (as if they aren't already—how often do they get to fill a cat litter box with cake?). Round off the ends so they are no longer blunt—you want them to look like they just came out of a cat. Bury your "droppings" in the cake mixture and repeat as many times as desired. Now take about 5 more rolls, preparing these as you have the others and set aside.

Sprinkle the other half of the cookie crumbs over the mixture.

Now take your last batch of Tootsie Rolls, and place them artfully on top. They are to look like fresh cat leavings. (I take one or two and drape them over the edge of the litter pan, in honor of Heidi, our tabby, who could never quite get her aim just right.)

Place the box on a newspaper and sprinkle the reserved ¼ cup cookie crumbs around the edge of the newspaper. (We do this in honor of Cinder, our black cat, who was vigorous in digging and scratching in the litter pan.)

Serve with a new Pooper Scooper.

DISMEMBERED-HAND PUNCH

2 latex gloves
1 (13-ounce) envelope unsweetened grape soft drink mix
1 (13-ounce) envelope unsweetened orange soft drink mix
2 cups sugar
3 quarts cold water
1 liter ginger ale

To make dismembered hands, wash 2 latex gloves (not powder-lined), fill with water, seal with rubber bands, and freeze until rock-hard.

Stir both the soft drink mixes together, then add the sugar and water until completely dissolved. The punch should be black in color.

Add some chilled ginger ale just before serving. Dip one of the frozen hands briefly in warm water, then peel off the glove. Float the dismembered hand in the punch bowl for a gruesome effect. Later, when it's time to refresh the punch bowl, you can add the other hand.

DECIDEDLY DREADFUL DECOR

Decorating for Halloween isn't about being cute or clever, but, rather, seeking to be repulsive and creepy. Check out the menu for inspiration—it will never earn you kudos on the Food Network. This stuff is positively vile—your guests are gonna love it!

The old dry-ice trick is something you have to do on your buffet table for a truly eerie effect. It's relatively easy to pull off. Just hide the dry ice by setting it in a roasting pan behind a large pumpkin. Pour hot water on the dry ice periodically and let it make its magic. Remember that dry ice emits a lot of carbon dioxide, so make sure you have this set up in a well-ventilated area. Remember, too, that you *never* touch dry ice: it will burn your skin. Always handle dry ice with big oven mitts to keep your skin out of harm's way.

For ease of accomplishment and to give the full effect of your truly repugnant buffet, make little note cards naming each item on the menu. This is simple to do on the computer, and if you use a creepy, drippy font, you'll further your ambience.

The Timeline

Really, the day before is adequate for everything, except the Bloody Eyeballs in Green Slime. In order to get your slime just right, you don't want the gelatin perfectly set and hard. You want it halfway set so it's a wonderfully glutinous, disgusting mess.

The cool part of this menu is that nothing needs to be done last minute, except perhaps, "igniting" as it were, the buffet's dry ice. And even though you could pull this whole menu off the day of your event, the gelatin portion of the Bloody Eyeballs in Green Slime really needs some good timing.

TWO WEEKS AHEAD

Send out invitations for your spooky affair.

ONE WEEK AHEAD

Check your kitchen tools and utensils against the recipe directions and buy or borrow anything you'll need.

THREE DAYS AHEAD

Clean out your refrigerator—you're going to need lots of room in there!

Check your pantry against your shopping list and head for the grocery store (with the list, of course).

Have your children carve their pumpkin.

Prepare "dismembered hands" according to recipe directions and store in freezer.

TWO DAYS AHEAD

Prepare and store Chocolate-covered Spiders (page 188).

Prepare and store Chopped Lizard Sandwiches (page 190).

Peel grapes and store in a zipper-topped plastic bag in the refrigerator.

Bake cupcakes (page 193); cool on a wire rack and store in large zipper-topped plastic bags.

Bake the two German chocolate cake mixes according to package directions, in two 9 × 13-inch pans; cool to room temperature, then cover and refrigerate.

Halloween is a $1.93 billion a year bonanza when it comes to the sale of candy, beating out Christmas, Easter, and Valentine's Day. One quarter of all the candy sold each year is purchased for Halloween.

Prepare pudding mix according to package directions; cover and refrigerate.

Process the Nilla Wafers in food processor according to recipe instructions, adding the green food coloring as instructed. Place all but ¼ cup in a large zipper-topped plastic bag. Place the ¼ cup in a small zipper-topped plastic bag. These can be stored in your pantry or refrigerator.

ONE DAY AHEAD

Prepare grape and orange soft drink mixes according to package directions; mix and store in large beverage containers in the refrigerator.

Assemble Dirt and Worm Cupcakes (page 193); cover and refrigerate.

SIX HOURS AHEAD

Prepare Barbecued Bat Wings (page 189).

THREE HOURS AHEAD

Assemble and arrange Kandi's Kitty Litter Cake (page 194).

TWO HOURS AHEAD

Prepare Cartilage and Blood-Clot Salad (page 191).

Prepare the lime gelatin for Bloody Eyeballs in Green Slime according to package directions, then peel the red grapes; set aside until lime gelatin is halfway to setting, then mix the grapes slightly into the gelatin.

JUST BEFORE SERVING

Add the peeled red grapes to the lime gelatin for Bloody Eyeballs in Green Slime.

Pull out all menu items and arrange on serving platters or bowls; place on table, displaying note cards with each item's recipe title on it.

Pour the chilled soft drink mixtures into punch bowl; add ginger ale and frozen "dismembered hands."

Arrange dry ice behind your carved pumpkin and "ignite" by pouring some hot water on it. (Do this periodically throughout the party.)
BOO!!!!!

A GROWN-UP
BIRTHDAY PARTY

We all remember playing Pin the Tail on the Donkey, blowing out the candles on a thickly iced birthday cake, and then digging into that same cake with gusto (and a scoop of vanilla ice cream, too). These are some of the nostalgic reminiscences of childhood birthday parties we all treasure in our hearts.

Well, there are still some memories to make, and now that you're an adult, it's time to make some doozies via a birthday party with a grown-up spin. So put on your party hat and let's make some noise! Birthdays are meant for celebrating, no matter what the age. Just because hitting a piñata for the explosion of candy no longer holds the allure it once did, that doesn't mean you have outgrown a birthday party. *Au contraire!* Tastes change (thank heavens) with maturity, and now instead of sappy party games, let's throw a surprise birthday party, with the birthday honoree's roasting, for a really fun evening. Let's get busy and Part-Tay!

Most everyone loves Mexican food. What's not to like? And for this casual, fun event, serving up a hefty helping of Hispanic home cooking is what this menu is all about.

MUSIC TO ROAST BY

You say it's your birthday. . . .
We're gonna have a good time . . .
—The Beatles

If you're going to roast the birthday boy, it's a good idea to have music to roast by. My suggestion is to make sure you have plenty of oldies mixed in with some new stuff. You can't beat the Beatles "Birthday Song" as the guest of honor enters the party! You'll also need a generous mix of Motown, rock, and some classic stuff, too—Frank Sinatra and Nat King Cole, for example. You want diverse and fun music. Stuff that evokes memories and stuff that's just plain fun to dance and listen to—a little disco and country boot kickin' music can do a body good, too.

A lot of this stuff can be had off the Internet in an MP3 download for pennies in comparison to heading to the music store and spending a small fortune buying all kinds of CDs. To get the mood right and really have a great party, you need to "choregraph" your party with the right music.

HOW TO HOST A ROAST

No need to search out sombreros, maracas, and a mariachi band (unless you want them). The menu might be Mexican, but the decor needs only to speak birthday and focus on the main thing: the guest of honor, whom you plan to roast lavishly. Go for bright festive colors, blow-up childhood pictures, embarrassing teenage prom pictures, and the like to rib your guest of honor and prepare him or her for the roast.

Naturally, each guest gets to put in his or her two cents and help with the roasting. Your invitations should include instructions on how long your guests should plan their "speeches" for the roast. Also, include some reminder that the speeches should be a gentle poke at the guest of honor, not an attempt to humiliate or embarrass. This is supposed to be fun, not mortifying.

Speaking of invitations, make the invitations fun, too. Have a baby picture of the guest of honor on top of the invitation with the pertinent information following: where, what, why, and when, as well as where to RSVP and the type of dress.

Tell the roastee to dress as if he were going to a formal event (fake him or her out and tell him you're going to dinner and the opera or something fancy) and then have all the guests show up really laid back and casual—in Hawaiian shirts, for example; this is a hilarious way to make your guest of honor really stand out.

▓ The Menu

GUACAMOLE, SALSA, AND CHIPS

SOFT TACO BAR

GRILLED SEASONED STEAK (OR CHICKEN)

   PICO DE GALLO

MEXICAN RICE PILAF

JALAPEÑO BLACK BEAN SALAD

GREEN SALAD WITH CILANTRO DRESSING

   AND PEPITAS

THE ULTIMATE CADILLAC MARGARITA

ASSORTED MEXICAN CERVEZAS (ASSORTED

   MEXICAN BEERS)

SHOPPING LIST

MEAT

6 pounds beef steak and/or boneless, skinless chicken
   breast halves

CONDIMENTS

Assorted jarred salsas (hot, medium, mild), for dipping

2 (24-ounce) jars salsa—your favorite, for cooking

Balsamic vinegar (3 cups)

Soy sauce (1½ cups)

Honey

Olive oil

Vegetable oil

Worcestershire sauce

Liquid Smoke

Low-fat mayonnaise

PRODUCE

9 to 10 ripe avocados

7 large limes

1 large red onion

2 medium red onions

2 small red onions

1 medium white onion

3 bunches cilantro

12 plum tomatoes

3 large tomatoes

3 heads garlic

2 bunches green onions

3 jalapeño peppers

1 small red bell pepper

4 heads romaine lettuce

CANNED GOODS

1 (14.5-ounce) can diced tomatoes

2 (14.5-ounce) cans low-sodium chicken broth

1 (15-ounce) can black beans

SPICES

Cayenne pepper

Ground cumin

Chili powder

Onion powder

Margarita salt

DAIRY/DAIRY CASE

Cheddar cheese (3 cups shredded)

Buttermilk (½ cup)

Sour cream

DRY GOODS

Sugar

Pepitas (Mexican pumpkin seeds)

Long-grain brown rice (2 cups)

FROZEN FOODS

1 (10-ounce) bag white corn kernels

BAKERY

3 dozen corn tortillas

Order a cake from a good bakery

OTHER

Gallon-size zipper-topped plastic bags

Plastic wrap

Tequila (Sauza Hornitos is a good brand)

Grand Marnier

Assorted Mexican cervezas (beers)

1 large bag tortilla chips

Birthday candles

Charcoal lighter or lighter fluid

TOOLS OF THE TRADE

Barbecue or grill

Barbecue tools

Food processor or blender

CHILE TODAY, HOT TAMALE

At last count, there are about a bazillion different types of chiles in the world. They vary greatly in both heat and flavor. For the most part, they add that bit of *caliente* we have all grown to love and identify with Mexican food.

Chiles have been around for thousands of years, both in the wild and cultivated. Capsaicin is an alkaloid found mostly in the white rib of the chile (this is how you deheat your chiles, by the way—by deribbing and deseeding). As a general rule, the smaller the chile, the hotter it is.

The Recipes

GUACAMOLE, SALSA, AND CHIPS

Serves 12

9 to 10 ripe avocados, peeled and pitted
2 large limes, juiced
1 teaspoon salt or to taste
1 large red onion, diced
½ cup chopped cilantro, or more to taste
6 plum tomatoes, diced
3 garlic cloves, pressed
Pinch of cayenne (optional)
1 jar salsa (your favorite variety)
1 large bag tortilla chips

In a large bowl, using a fork, mash together the avocados, lime juice, and salt. Mix in the onion, cilantro, tomatoes, and garlic. Stir in the cayenne if you choose to use it. For best flavor, serve immediately and don't refrigerate. Place the avocado seed in the middle to keep mixture from turning brown, and remove just before you serve, then give the guacamole a quick stir. Serve with salsa and tortilla chips.

SOFT TACO BAR

This really couldn't get any easier. The whole idea is to have lots of stuff chopped up and ready to go. The Taco Bar works well for everyone —vegetarians or chicken and steak lovers alike. Read the list of stuff you can have on your bar and choose what you would like or, better yet, have it all!

Grilled Seasoned Steak (or Chicken) (page 206), cut into strips
Jalapeño Black Bean Salad (page 209)
Chopped green onions
Chopped red onions
Chopped cilantro
Chopped plum tomatoes
Sour cream
Salsa (an assortment of jarred salsas: hot, medium, and mild)
Pico de Gallo (page 207)
Romaine lettuce, chopped
Shredded Cheddar cheese
Warmed corn tortillas

GRILLED SEASONED STEAK (OR CHICKEN)

Serves 12 (makes enough for 6 pounds of meat)

It's this marinade that will make your meat or poultry go from tasty to spectacular. This works great for both meat and chicken; however, separate them when marinating if you want to do both.

> *3 cups balsamic vinegar*
> *1½ cups soy sauce*
> *2 heads garlic, pressed*
> *¾ cup honey*
> *¾ cup olive oil*
> *1 tablespoon each Worcestershire sauce, onion powder, and black pepper (preferably freshly ground pepper)*
> *1 tablespoon salt*
> *2 teaspoons Liquid Smoke (available by the Worcestershire sauce, usually)*
> *¼ teaspoon cayenne*

Mix all the ingredients in a large bowl.

Place your meat and/or chicken in large plastic bag(s) (remember—two separate bags if you're going to be doing both chicken and meat). Pour in the marinade and close securely. Place the bags in the fridge overnight, but no longer than two days.

Preheat your grill to medium-high heat.

Grill the meat and/or chicken about 5 to 7 minutes per side, or until cooked through. Discard the marinade. (It's full of all kinds of yucky cooties now and needs to go!)

Let the meat cool enough to handle, then cut on an angle into strips and serve on platters.

PICO DE GALLO

Makes 2 cups

3 large ripe tomatoes, diced
1 small red onion, finely chopped
½ fresh jalapeño pepper, seeded, deribbed, and chopped
½ cup finely chopped cilantro
Salt and pepper to taste

Mix everything in a large bowl. Refrigerate till ready to use.

Take out mixture about ½ hour before serving time so it can warm up a bit. It tastes better closer to room temperature rather than cold. The tomato flavor really pops.

MEXICAN RICE PILAF

Serves 12

1 tablespoon vegetable oil
1 medium white onion, chopped
2 cups long-grain rice
¾ teaspoon ground cumin
½ teaspoon chili powder
⅔ cup canned diced tomatoes (with juice)
Salt and pepper to taste
3¼ cups low-sodium chicken broth

In a large saucepan, heat the oil over medium heat till hot. Add the onion and sauté till soft and translucent, about 5 minutes.

Pour the rice into the pan and stir to coat rice, then mix in the rest of the ingredients, cover, bring to a boil, and reduce heat to low. Simmer for 20 to 30 minutes or until rice is tender and liquid is absorbed. Stir occasionally to prevent sticking and remember, too, that pilaf could be done earlier than the recipe says because some stovetops run hotter than others.

JALAPEÑO BLACK BEAN SALAD

Serves 12

1 (10-ounce) bag frozen white corn, thawed

1 (15-ounce) can black beans, rinsed and drained

1 small red onion, diced

1 small red bell pepper, deseeded, deribbed, and chopped

6 green onions, chopped

2 jalapeño peppers, seeded, deribbed, and finely chopped

1 (24-ounce) jar salsa

2 tablespoons ground cumin

Salt and pepper to taste

2 tablespoons sugar

½ cup finely chopped cilantro

In a large bowl, gently stir all the ingredients together. Refrigerate for at least 1 hour (can be made ahead).

GREEN SALAD WITH CILANTRO DRESSING AND PEPITAS

Serves 12

1 cup fresh cilantro, stems and leaves
½ cup buttermilk
½ cup low-fat mayonnaise
2 pinches of sugar
3 heads of romaine, chopped
½ cup pepitas (Mexican pumpkin seeds)

In a food processor or blender, combine the cilantro, buttermilk, mayonnaise, and sugar. Cover and process until smooth.

Before serving, toss the greens with the dressing and top with the pepitas.

THE ULTIMATE CADILLAC MARGARITA

Serves 4

You need to think outside the blender if you're going to make amazing margaritas. They should be stirred, not shaken (violently in a blender). So toss your blender aside for these margaritas. Once you've driven a Cadillac, you'll never go back.

> *4 limes, zested and juiced*
> *¼ cup sugar*
> *3 tablespoons water*
> *1 cup premium tequila (I like Sauza Hornitos)*
> *2 tablespoons Grand Marnier*
> *1 lime, sliced into rounds*
> *Margarita salt, for those who like it*

In a bowl, combine the lime zest and juice, sugar, and water. Cover and refrigerate for approximately 24 hours.

Add to this mixture the tequila and Grand Marnier. Rub the rims of 4 glasses with sliced lime and dip into salt (or for a Topless Ultimate Cadillac Margarita, forgo the salt). Add ice and pour the margaritas over the top.

THE BIRTHDAY SONG

You know that song, you've sung it a zillion times—the traditional birthday song sung just before the candles are blown out. Did you know that it started as a song for teachers to greet the children as they came into the classroom? Two Kentucky sisters, Mildred and Patty Hill, passionate educators, gave teachers this song:

> Good morning to you
> Good morning to you
> Good morning dear children
> Good morning to all.

It wasn't until about 1924 that the lyrics were changed for birthdays and the song began being sung traditionally at birthday gatherings.

The Timeline

THREE WEEKS AHEAD

Plan your decor and music, and design your invitations. If you need any photos reproduced, this is the time to have them processed.

TWO WEEKS AHEAD

Send your invitations. Be sure to let your guests know this is a *surprise*!

ONE WEEK AHEAD

Check your kitchen tools and utensils against the recipe directions and buy or borrow anything you'll need.

Check your inventory of serving pieces, particularly glasses for margaritas and bowls for the taco bar.

Order your birthday cake.

TWO DAYS AHEAD

Clean out your refrigerator.

Check your pantry against your shopping list and then go shopping.

ONE DAY AHEAD

Prepare the marinade and marinate steak and/or chicken in (separate) large zipper-topped plastic bags; store in refrigerator.

Prepare the Jalapeño Black Bean Salad (page 209); cover and refrigerate.

Prepare the Soft Taco Bar (page 205) ingredients, *except tortillas*, and store in individual zipper-topped plastic bags in the refrigerator.

Prepare the dressing for Green Salad with Cilantro Dressing and Pepitas (page 210); cover and store in refrigerator.

Wash and chop romaine lettuce for salad; store in large plastic bags in refrigerator.

Prepare the Pico de Gallo (page 207); cover and refrigerate.

THE DAY OF

Draft someone to pick up the cake.

ONE-HALF HOUR AHEAD

Pull Pico de Gallo from refrigerator and bring to room temperature.

Prepare Mexican Rice Pilaf (page 208).

Prepare Guacamole (page 204).

Arrange tortilla chips in a napkin-lined basket.

Pour jarred salsa into a small serving bowl.

Arrange sliced limes and margarita salt on a tray with the tequila and Grand Marnier, and make sure beers are cooling in the fridge.

JUST BEFORE SERVING

Toss the chopped romaine lettuce with the chilled dressing and add pepitas.

Remove the avocado seed from the Guacamole and give it a final stir. If you plan to do so, arrange it on a tray with salsa and tortilla chips.

Warm the corn tortillas; then arrange with other ingredients for Soft Taco Bar.

Pull the Black Bean Salad from refrigerator and arrange on table.

Transfer the cooked Mexican Rice Pilaf to a serving bowl and place on table.

INDEX

LEANNE ELY is considered *the* expert on family cooking and healthy eating. She is a certified nutritionist, public speaker, and the host of savingdinner.com. Leanne has a weekly "Food for Thought" column on the ever-popular Flylady.net website, as well as her own e-zine, *Healthy Foods*, which has been published weekly for the past four years. She lives in North Carolina with her two teenaged children.

ABOUT THE TYPE

This book was set in Goudy, a typeface designed by Frederic William Goudy (1865–1947). Goudy began his career as a bookkeeper, but devoted the rest of his life to the pursuit of "recognized quality" in a printing type.

Goudy was produced in 1914 and was an instant bestseller for the foundry. It has generous curves and smooth, even color. It is regarded as one of Goudy's finest achievements.